M000196157

Mo' Dave Trippin

More Day Trips in the Appalachian Galaxy of
Ohio, Kentucky, West Virginia and Beyond

Dave Lavender

photography by Toril Lavender

Copyright © 2015 Lavender Publishing

All rights reserved.

ISBN: 0-9801766-2-X
ISBN-13: 978-0-9801766-2-9

DEDICATION

Dave Trippin is dedicated to our first travel mates - Dave's sisters Cindy, Jen and Cats and Toril's brothers Tim and Aaron with whom we've shared a thousand adventures and sore knuckles from playing 'Slug Bug.'
We also dedicate the book to everyone who bought the first book and inspired us with their own tales, postcards and photos from the road.

TABLE OF CONTENTS

ACKNOWLEDGMENTS

Dave Trippin would like to thank Ed Dawson and The Herald-Dispatch for continuing to support our family-fueled travel series. We would like to thank Richard Bartram for the inspiration for the cover, and to artist Thom Marsh for the original Dave Trippin caricature. Also, a big thanks to kindred traveling spirits near and far who've kept kindly peppering us with questions as to when the next Dave Trippin was coming out.

INTRODUCTION

Gee how time flies when you are having fun, and volunteering like mad for just about everything - PTSO, band boosters, Boy Scouts, the GHS alumni association - you name it and we are signed up for it.

Toss in an after-school gardening program, playing in a band, the chaotic work of the newspaper and freelance photography business, and trying to keep a family of growing boys fed and somehow days dissolve into nights.

We blinked and somehow it has been seven years since our first travel book, "Dave Trippin: A Daytripper's Guide to the Appalachian Galaxy of Ohio, Kentucky and West Virginia," was published. And thank the dear Lord in heaven for gracious readers, it has been five years since the book has been sold out. That has saved us from having to madly search Pinterest for what to do with crates of unread books.

In the years since, the boys (Jake and Will) mere babes in the first book's tales, are full-on man cubs. Jake "Trombone Red" is taller than me, wearing clothes (including my jeans jacket from 1989) and is on the wild journey that is high school.

Will is in middle school where he plays soccer, is in Scouts and has mastered the art of the eye roll while looking at his parents.

Like the first book, this Dave Trippin (written from 2015 back to 2008) is a collection of our mostly newspaper-published series known for its candid recall of our family's fun. It is sometimes dysfunctional and dangerous and hopefully always interesting and full of adventure that we hope you too can check out.

With summer's shrinking like a plastic bag thrown in a fire (oh the things you learn on Scout trips), we try to get away when we can with annual Spring Break trips, and long-weekends. We've explored our little slice of the world through a host of festivals from the Snowy Luau and Civil War reenactments to the wild Winter Adventure Weekend where we have crawled the world's largest cardboard cave and rappelled off a cliff through a natural bridge.

We hope you have as much fun as we did doing some of these trips, and only half the trouble.

Stay in touch with us on our Dave Trippin Facebook page and as they say at Winter Adventure Weekend, "Keep Calm and Adventure On."

Kentucky

SHAKER VILLAGE

There's two kinds of people in this kinetic world — movers and Shakers.

While it's mission impossible to track down the first group since they're always well, moving, as for the Shakers — we know where they live or at least used to — just a couple hours west of Huntington and right in the heart of central Kentucky's horse country is Shaker Village of Pleasant Hill.

While there are only three Shakers left in the U.S. living up at Sabbathday Lake in Maine, you can learn everything you ever wanted to know about one of America's larger intentional communities in a weekend exploring the gorgeous and sprawling Shaker Village whose mission is to preserve 34 original buildings and 3,000 acres of countryside once overrun with these remarkable believers.

Although I had since my bluegrass gospel singing days in college sworn off worshipping with church folks one shake, rattle and holy roll away from an EMS call, the Dave Trippin' mobile found itself in the heart of all things Shaker a few weeks back.

Our oldest boy is in Huntington Middle School's Western Virginia Military Academy (one of the only school-age Civil War reenacting units in the nation) and they and the lovely hooped-dress-wearing gals of the Lizzie Cabell Finishing School For Young Ladies (also at HMS), were all invited to take part in the Village's Civil War Weekend called "Troops At Our Door Step: The Civil War Marches Through Shaker Village."

While you dear reader don't have to sleep on the ground in itchy wool eating hard tack to soak in the ambiance of the Village, I do recommend visiting soon.

Although Shaker Village is open year-round and is packed with events (including a month-long historic holiday event in December), I must say that sliver of horse country is truly almost heaven as the leaves change along the windy, stone-fenced roads leading to the Village.

And hey, October is also the **Fall Meet at Keeneland** (1-800-456-3412, www.keeneland.com), which is so close to Shaker Village you could throw a rock and hit it, which the Shakers would be doing were they still around.

Packed with a super-sized heirloom garden filled with such Shaker oddities as salsify (an odd root veg that doesn't taste like chicken but that folks swear tastes like oysters), the Village again is bustling with fall events showcasing the bounty of the harvest of life as it was - and is recreated - down on the Farm.

One of those September fall favorites is the Shaker Village "Harvest Fest," that features a kids village Farm Olympics, sheep shearing and herding, u-pick apples and pumpkins, hay rides, a hay climb, a best dessert competition, live music and much more.

As part of Harvest Fest, there's also The Heirloom Supper as well as the Harvest 5-Mile Trail Run on Saturday.

There's also a Spirit Stroll to the Graveyard every Friday and Saturday evening in the fall as well as special Fall on the Farm weekends that take place from 10 a.m. to 5 p.m. every Saturday in October.

Thanks to a dedicated legion of costumed reenactors (such as Susan Hughes who invited long-time reenacting friend Mike Sheets and his HMS students down for the weekend) the Shaker Village comes to life for visitors who once inside the sprawling compound are free to roam down the tree-lined graveled path (that was once Route 68) where history shakes alive with songs, dance, detailed talk of Shaker architecture and of the sect's progressive social stances on equality.

For folks like me who won't be selecting "19th Century Religious Sects" as a topic on Jeopardy, the United Society of Believers in Christ or Shakers were a branch of the Quakers who came to America from England in the 1770s following Mother Ann Lee, who believed Christ was coming back as a woman and that the road to salvation was more easily traveled thanks to constant confession and celibacy - a welcome respite for many pioneer women who could easily have 8 or 9 kids by the time they were in their 20s.

Amazingly, in this country that still doesn't have a law for

equal pay for women, the Shakers in the 18th and 19th centuries not only believed but practiced equality for women and all races (including African-Americans whose brethren and sisters were slaves on every other surrounding Kentucky farm).

Thinking they were living in Heaven on Earth (which many central Kentuckians and thoroughbreds living in million dollar barns nearby would amen), the Shakers grew to 500 residents living and working side by side in some 260 structures at the 4,500-acre Pleasant Hill by the mid 1800s.

Kentucky's Shaker Village was the third largest of 19 societies in the U.S. However, since "celibate good times" although snappy, isn't the most sustainable slogan for any group, the Shakers found

themselves dwindling as social attitudes changed and the wheels of the Industrial Revolution helped further unhinge the group.

By 1910 Shaker Village at Pleasant Hill was closed and in 1920, the last Shaker who had lived at Pleasant Hill (one of two Kentucky Shaker settlements) passed away.

Historic restoration begin in 1961 to help preserve part of the sprawling village and the Shakers' unique quest for the simple and true gifts of life.

While it indeed is just a shadow of its former self, what an unforgettable shadow it is.

Unlike some staid historic sites, Shaker Village teems with dozens of ways to experience the simple treasures of the Shaker life and the abundant beauty of Central Kentucky's rolling hills and farmlands from horse-drawn wagon rides by Blue and Ivy the Percheron draft horses to rides on the Dixie Belle Riverboat that slow paddles its way through the Kentucky River Palisades and under High Bridge, an engineering marvel built in 1877.

For folks who want a vacation from their devices, a stay in one of the cottages such as the Old Ministry Shop or The Inn at Shaker Village and its 70 rooms may suffice.

Although be forewarned that things there do go bump in the night. On our trip, the Looneys, who in spite of their name are not crazy but who seem to attract spirits since Stephan created the iGhostHunter app, kept getting phone calls throughout the night. No big deal, except, no one was on the line and the lady at the front desk said yeah they are coming from a part of Shaker Village that no longer exists. She also nonchalantly cited the fact that the Shaker spirits didn't care for any Civil War reenactors since troops from both sides had swarmed the pacifist village in the 1860s,.

Downstairs in the Inn, is the Trustees' Office Dining Room, a favorite regional restaurant that serves up piles of veg from the nearby garden including salsify casserole, relish bowls, fried chicken, and other Kentucky after-dinner favorites like chess pie. While it is easy to overindulge in the garden bounty, it's also easy to walk off a great meal there.

The 3,000-acre Nature Preserve at Shaker Village has three sets of trails (for walking and horse trail riding), and right out the steps of the restaurant puts you on the delightfully quaint gravel road - a ribbon through the heart of the village and to its many barns, shops, meeting places and museums, including the must-see 40-room Centre Family Dwelling that was the second largest structure in the Commonwealth (next to the Capitol) when it was built in 1824.

You can explore the four-floor building on your own, but costumed interpreters also give guided tours and are often milling about ready to answer questions on the Shaker's legacy in traditional crafts from their world-famous furniture designs to their unique oval wooden boxes and broom making.

No visit to Shaker Village is complete without a visit to the Meeting House where interpreters such as the incredible Donna Philips (the music coordinator) share the sometimes whimsical and often wild dances of the sect, and a few (thankfully not too many) of the more than 20,000 songs in the Shaker songbook giving folks a divine taste of a church service both shaken and stirred.

It was hard for me to imagine with just one little lady snorting and singing and boot-pounding the floor but in its heyday 500 folks pounded these wood floors here roaring for the Lord - a rumbling heard dozens of miles away in the 1800s.

Somehow in a war-spun world often only filled with ringing sounds, the rumbling of the Shaker's peaceful gift of a true and simple life can still be heard and it's only a day trip away.

Let's Go Trippin: Shaker Village

WHAT: Shaker Village of Pleasant Hill, a non-profit national historic landmark preserving 34 original buildings and 3,000 acres of countryside inhabited by the Shakers from 1805 until about 1910.

WHERE: 3501 Lexington Road, Harrodsburg, Ky., (south of Lexington) and about three hours west of Huntington.

DINING: The Trustees' Office Dining Room features traditional and seasonal Kentucky dishes inspired by ingredients (including rare plants such as Salsify) in the Shaker's garden. Served daily except for Christmas Eve and Christmas Day.

STAYING WITH THE SHAKERS: The Inn at Shaker Village features more than 70 rooms, with Shaker reproduction furniture, and there are also suites and cottages in 13 Shaker buildings.

WHAT TO DO: Explore the history at the Historic Centre, The Farm, The Preserve (which has 40 miles of multi-use trails) and overnight stable facilities for folks who bring their horse to ride the grounds.

ON THE RIVER: Head to the Shaker Landing at the Kentucky River where they operate they operate the 115-passenger paddlewheeler, The Dixie Belle, which runs the cliff-lined Palisades section of the Kentucky River. Learn how the Shakers used to venture as far as New Orleans to trade seeds, brooms, preserves and livestock. You can also do a DIY paddle trip but there is a $5 launch fee at the Landing.

SPECIAL WEEKENDS: Enjoy wildflower hikes, primitive skill workshops, spring waterfall photography hikes, trail runs, homeschool day, Harvest Fest and much more.

DID YOU KNOW? The BBC named Shaker Village of Pleasant Hill as a top hidden travel destination.

CONTACT: Go online at www.shakervillageky.org or call 1-800-734-5611

Heritage Farm Museum and Village: Located at 3300 Harvey Road, Huntington, has guided tours Monday through Saturday, and has artisans working year-round. The national award-winning museum and pioneer village comes to life on the first Saturday of

every month from May to December for the Way Back Weekend. Go online at www.heritagefarmmuseum.com.

Guyandotte Civil War Days: Celebrating its 26th anniversary in 2015, the Civil War Days, which runs the first weekend in November, features hundreds of costumed Civil War enthusiasts doing living history portrayals. Come out and hear nightly presentations on Civil War history in the region, take one of the nightly Civil War haunted tours. Stop by the camps where experts in everything from battlefield medicine to local history give personal tours. The Madie Carroll House, which survived the town's burning during the Civil War is also open then for tours. Go online at www.guyandottecivilwarsdays.com.

West Virginia Pumpkin Festival: One of the highlights of the West Virginia Pumpkin Festival (held every first October weekend)

is its super-sized pioneer encampment. Middle Creek Station's wood-smoke and living history-filled encampment has been a West Virginia Pumpkin Festival crowd favorite since the fest began 30 years ago. Stop by Middle Creek Station and watch and learn from Red Dog and the rest of the two-dozen-strong West Augusta Volunteers' bring the settlement to life with the sights, sounds and smells of cast-iron cooking, apple-pressing, tomahawk throwing, lye-soap making, spinning, blacksmithing, leatherworking, fiddling and much more. Check out Middle Creek Station's FB page for more info.

Wolfpen Woods: Wolfpen Woods Pioneer Village, LLC., is located at 20740 Wolfpen Woods, Rush, Ky. Just outside of Ashland, take a trip back to pioneer days as you can see a re-enactment of life during the 1790s to 1820s on special weekends like the Indian Summer 18th Century Living History, and the annual Heritage Harvest Tour. Go online at www.wolfpenwoods.com for more info.

Pioneer Life Week: Running July 20-26 in 2015, Pioneer Life Week at Carter Caves State Resort Park is a full week dedicated to the Revolutionary War, The War of 1812 and the settlement of lands around the Ohio River, re-enactors, musical entertainment and many historical programs bring this rich heritage back to life. Historical programs are scheduled daily throughout the week including tomahawk throwing, black powder rifle demonstrations, spinning and weaving demonstrations, 18th century poultry care, primitive fire making, atlatl demonstrations, pioneer clothing interpretation and a County Fair Day. Call 606-286-4411 for more info.

Woodland Cemetery Tour: Taking place usually on the last Saturday in September, the Ironton Woodland Ghost Walk is put on by the Lawrence County Historical Society. Cone out for a historical walk to encounter living history portrayals of Underground Railroad Conductors, Iron Masters, Ballerina's, Civil

War Veterans etc. Approximately 75 people will portray various individuals buried there. People are encouraged to bring a flash light and comfortable walking shoes.

Ashland Cemetery Tour: In its 14th year in 2015, Dining With the Past is a living history event put on by the Highlands Museum and Discovery Center in Ashland long with the Friends of Ashland Cemetery. Held in October, enjoy guided tours of the historic Ashland Cemetery, connecting visitors with the men and women who founded the city, as well as businesses throughout our region. Visitors will hear stories from individuals such as Ashland Poage, a founding family member; Walter Franz, who was killed in the Battle of the Bulge in WWII; Paul Blazer, founder of Ashland Oil; and Mary Elliott Flannery, the first woman to be elected to the Kentucky General Assembly. The tours often include refreshments and dinner at the museum. Go online at www.highlandsmuseum.com for more info.

Point Pleasant Reenactments: Home to Fort Randolph and Tu-Endie-Wei, Point Pleasant, where the Revolutionary War Battle of Point Pleasant raged, is home to several pioneer/Native American living history weekends including one of the largest in the region October's Battle Days, which reenacts the famous battle of 1774 that killed the famous Shawnee chief Cornstalk. Go online at www.masoncountytourism.org

Blennerhassett Island Historical State Park: Take a sternwheeler over to Blennerhassett Island, home to the restored mansion of Herman and Margaret Blennerhassett, who built a 7,000 square foot home (one of the largest in America in 1800) that they had to fell in 1806 after they became entangled with the Aaron Burr expedition. Now a state park, the island and its restored home draws about 50,000 visitors a year. Special events include a Civil War reenactment, lectures, evening cruises, the famous candlelight tour, and many other special events with living history portrayals. The park runs May through October. There's also bicycle rentals, wagon rides and primitive camping on the island. Go online at http://www.blennerhassettislandstatepark.com

Kentucky

RED RIVER GORGE

With the kids off recently for spring break, the Dave Trippin' crew figured it was high time to make a break for the golden arches.

Back off Jamie Oliver, we're not talking about driving through McDonald's. We're talking about soaking up some real golden arches -- catching a priceless sunset in the Red River Gorge, home to more than 200 natural bridges and arches, and a slew of unusual rock formations.

Located just two hours southwest of Huntington, **the Red River Gorge** (www.redrivergorge.com, 606-663-1161), is a wonder-filled world away. Home to the most arches east of the Rocky Mountains, it's an outdoor lovers paradise that is also home to the Red River National Wild and Scenic River, the Red River Gorge Geological Area (home to some of the best rock climbing in the east), Natural Bridge State Resort Park (one of Kentucky's first state parks), and a bevy of quirky attractions that includes the Kentucky Reptile Zoo, one of the world's largest collections of venomous snakes.

You can leave Huntington and be sitting on the skylift at Natural Bridge in two hours by Jeff Gordon-ing west from I-64 to the Mountain Parkway at Winchester where you cut south. But perhaps because I was, seriously, raised on the Back Road, over in Franklin Furnace, Ohio, I've always been a fan of the road less traveled.

We zipped off I-64 at the Farmers exit (just pass Morehead) and slowly snaked our way southwest down to the Gorge driving west of Cave Run, and for the most part rolling through some of

the expansive (707,000-acre) **Daniel Boone National Forest** (http://www.fs.usda.gov/dbnf) through such little tree-lined towns as Salt Lick and Frenchburg.

Between Morehead and the Gorge we saw all kinds of Charles Kuralt kind of cool: an old roller rink, three mules pulling a plow, a sign to the Menifee County skate park and read it now and believe it later but a road-side yard sign that read "Piano For Sale -- House Also."

You can't find any of that on an interstate, and best of all there were no miles of orange construction barrels.

Along the way, we quit counting the amazing number of quilt blocks that now grace barns threading through the backroads of Rowan, Bath and Menifee counties thanks to **Kentucky's Quilt Trail.** (Route your own path to the blocks at (http://artscouncil.ky.gov/KentuckyArt/QTrails.htm)

Maybe it was the chugging of the fresh Ale-8-1's, the Winchester, Ky.-made official drink of eastern Kentucky, but I got almost electric inside knowing our friend, Donna Sue Groves, up in Adams County, Ohio, had birthed this National Quilt Barn Trail in 2001 to pay homage to her quilt-making mama, and -- although she is in tough fight with breast cancer -- has lived to see her love grow and spread so beautifully all over the country in 42 states with thousands of quilt blocks from Texas to three new ones in old Central City.

Taking Ky. 77 south and slicing into the Gorge we didn't need a

GPS to know when we'd arrived in Kentucky's Rockies as the setting went from those beautiful, rolling Kentucky hills with barns, ponds and Bradford pears to towering, sheer sandstone cliffs and odd-shaped, house-sized boulders strewn about like there had been some ancient clash of the titans.

Cars parked along the **Red River Geological Area** (www.redrivergorge.com) were getting a little more exotic than Powell County license plates. Just in one parking lot there were rockclimbers' cars from Ontario, Massachusetts and Indiana.

And roadside attractions were popping up as well. Thank God for small favors, but the **Kentucky Reptile Zoo** (606-663-9160), and its collection of slithering serpents, was not yet open for the season.

Whew, we hauled dust out of there while Will exclaimed "the only thing that would scare me is bird-eating spiders and piranhas."

Yeah, right.

Needing a homebase for our Red River excursions we rolled on Kentucky 11 to **Natural Bridge State Resort Park**, 2135 Natural Bridge Road, Slade, Ky. (606-663-2214) to spend a couple nights.

Home to more than 20 miles of trails, two lakes, and the massive Natural Bridge, the 78-foot-long and 65-foot-tall arch, Natural Bridge has been drawing in tourists since Daniel Boone wandered by in 1767.

Since we, uh, didn't pack our rock-climbing shoes, we thought we might take a little easier way to the top.

Around since 1967, the 1/2-mile-long **Skylift at Natural Bridge** (606-663-2922, open April through October) is a fantastic way to the see some of the cliffs, and as we did, you can take the 22-minute-long ride one-way for only $6, and hike back down.

The price of a one-way ticket to access most of the park's web of nine interconnected trails was more than worth it, and along the way I got to enjoy the funny ramblings of Will, our first grader in deep woods thought who said, "Sometimes standing and sitting is doing something. You can't do nothing. Doing nothing is doing something."

Amen little buddy since we are currently sitting yet listening to treetops sighing and wind whispering and birds singing and don't look now but we are going straight up a sheer sandstone cliff.

While we got amazing views, I can't imagine how gorgeous it all is when the massive thickets of mountain laurel bloom in late May or in October when these hills are covered in the color quilt of fall.

Once at the top, it's only 600 feet to see what they oddly-enough still bill as "Kentucky's best-kept secret" -- Natural Bridge.

While doubting how well Kentuckians can keep a secret since Natural Bridge has been a public park since the Lexington and Eastern Railroad opened the area in 1896, and a state park since 1926, we were all impressed with their ability to share such awe-inspiring natural beauty.

Because of spring break, the Hemlock Lodge was filled to the brim, and with early April temps touching into the 80s, throngs of smiling families packed the main trails to and from the Natural Bridge and that included such odd portions as the tight-squeeze at Fat Man's Misery leading underneath the arch.

In two days of hiking, we found the park tailor made for families as the majority of hikes aren't that long, but all feature spectacular surprises. Ditto for the nearby **Red River Gorge Geological Area**, where spectacular sites such as Angel Windows and Sky Bridge are just a short hike to breathtaking beauty.

While dining at the Hemlock Lodge, we heard a waitress describe the proximity as "where that parking lot ends the trail begins," and she was right on. The Original Trail, the park's oldest trail, and easiest to the Natural Bridge, is just a stone's throw outside the lodge.

Built in the 1890s, it's a wonderful walk through history as it features four trail shelters, including two Civilian Conservation Corps shelters from the 1930s, on your way up through impressive thickets of rhododendron and to the top of the Natural Bridge. A great and short (0.75-mile) loop back is Balanced Rock Trail that leads past a sheer sandstone cliff called Rocky Point and down a steep series of stairs to the well-named hunk of sandstone on a pedestal known as Balanced Rock. Toss in a cave for good luck, and it's a perfect kid trail that makes a great loop with The Original Trail.

While we loved the amazing trail system at Natural Bridge with such great trails as Rock Garden Trail, Battleship Rock, Laurel Ridge and Low Gap, an early April forecast into the 90s sent us scurrying for the nearest water hole on our second day in the Gorge.

In summer season, there's little reason to leave **Natural Bridge SRP** (606-663-2214) as there's a good-sized swimming pool that sits below Hemlock Lodge and across from the famous Hoedown Island, a concert area surrounded by the lake. Named the Clogging Capital of Kentucky, Hoedown Island brings the square dancing and clogging thunder with as many as 500 folks gathering every Saturday until Memorial Day, every Friday and Saturday through Labor Day, then every Saturday through October.

But since it was early and Natural Bridge SRP didn't have any canoe excursions planned for the nearby Red River, a National Wild and Scenic River, we started dialing up the two canoe liveries **Red River Outdoors**, 415 Natural Bridge Road, Slade (859-230-3567) and **Red River Adventures** (606-663-1012) to see if we could rent a canoe for the day.

While the upper stretches of the Red is little wild with a decent stretch of Class III rapids (not commercially run), we packed a lunch and lit out on 8-mile unguided float with a canoe and kayak, a milder ride but still flowing through the heart of the rocky playground that is the Gorge.

We swam, fished, hunted for fossils, stopped, skipped rocks, looked and listened in silence to the frolicking frogs, those spring peepers singing their song of love, and together a great hot day melted away.

After a day on the river, and the boys singing a surround-sound chorus of "hungry," we pulled over to the almost-famous hangout, **Miguel's Pizza** (606-663-1975), the hippie soul kitchen and rock-climbing heart of the Gorge.

Coated in bright yellow and green paint like it's straight out of Nogales, the funky little restaurant serves fresh, organic meals while also selling all things climbing from ropes and chalk to new rock climbing shoes.

While waiting for a garlic, mushroom and artichoke pesto pizza and a Feta cheese and hot bacon salad, we guzzled some more Ale-8's, and had a ball shooting baskets in the gravel basketball court out back and trying the tightrope walking that was stretched between two trees in the front of Miguel's spacious campground full of rock-climbers from a dozen states.

When the meal came it was time for a blessing and a clink of the green glass of the Ale-8's.

After a long winter that's chewed enough potholes into Huntington streets to make the Pope cuss, it's been all too easy to complain about the weather and the water and the wind and the erosion around us.

But after a couple days of sunset hikes at Angel Windows, Sky Bridge and Natural Bridge it's a bit easier to give it up for Mother Nature's chisels, and to drink an Ale-8 toast to the sandstone art of wasting away so close to home.

Let's Go Trippin: Red River Gorge

WHERE TO STAY: Natural Bridge State Resort Park in Slade, Ky. The park has 35 rooms (with private balcony views) at its Hemlock Lodge, Natural Bridge also has four two-bedroom, or seven one-bedroom cottages and two campgrounds, Whittleton Campground and Middle Fork Campground, combining for 87 sites with utilities. Call 606-663-2214. Go online at parks.ky.gov and click onto Natural Bridge. There are also about a dozen places that rent private cabins, and about half a dozen campgrounds including Miguel's, a restaurant, campground, and rock climbing information center near the park. Call 606-663-1975.

Sky Bridge Station in Pine Ridge, Ky., has a bar and grill, gear and overnight accommodations. There's two bedrooms with 11 beds. Cost is $17 per bed or $70 per room. Call 606-668-9927.

GETTING THERE: Natural Bridge is exactly two hours southwest of Huntington. Take I-64 west to Winchester, Ky., take the Bert T. Combs Mountain Parkway to Slade, Ky. Take Kentucky 11 to the park.

WHAT ELSE: The Kentucky Reptile Zoo, 200 L&E Railroad Road, Slade, Ky. Open 11 a.m. to 6 p.m. daily in the summer and 11 a.m. to 6

p.m. Friday through Sundays in spring and fall. One of the world's largest collections of venomous snakes. Call 606-663-9160.

Torrent Falls Climbing Adventure, 1617 Ky. 11, Campton, Ky. Torrent Falls is the first via ferrata climbing facility in the U.S. with iron hand and foot runs that aid climbers as they scale rock faces. Call 606-668-6613 or go online at torrentfalls.com. For a complete list of cool things to do from Meadowgreen Music Hall to the Mountain View Drive-In Theater and the Mountain Park Dragway, go online at www.kyrockies.com or call 606-663-1161.

ON THE WATER: Natural Bridge SRP hosts some canoe day-trips on the nearby Red River, a National Wild and Scenic River. There are also two canoe liveries offering rentals as well as shuttles. Red River Outdoors, 415 Natural Bridge Road, Slade, offers canoeing, rock climbing, paintball and cabins. Call 859-230-3567 or online at www.redriveroutdoors.com. Red River Adventures, on the river at the junction of 715 and 77, has canoe rentals, camping and concessions. Call 606-663-1012 or go online at www.redriveradventure.net.

SCENIC ROUTE IN THE GORGE: The Red River Gorge National Scenic Byway is a curvy, small road that snakes through the heart of the Gorge and its breathtaking geological features, waterfalls, arches, the River and history. The Byway also includes the amazing Nada Tunnel. The Clifty Wilderness Area, and the Gladie Creek Historic Site and Learning Center. Go online at www.tourseky.com for more info.

More Cool Bridges

OK, Red River Gorges' bridges are all natural. But here's a look at a few cool manmade bridges in the region.

Bridges of Ritter Park: In Huntington's Ritter Park (named a Top 10 public space in America), go west from the 13th Street shelter along the PATH along Fourpole Creek. Enjoy a series of tiny, old bridges spanning the small creek. Go online at www.geocaching.com to begin the hunt for several geocaches near these bridges. Go online at www.ghprd.org for more info.

Rotary Park Bridge: Built in 1929-30, during the era of the CCC and WPA, the stone bridge at Rotary Park in Huntington is on the National Register of Historic Places. The 175-foot-long and 30-foot-wide bridge is made of native rock-faced, square-cut ashlar in a rustic style. You can place it on the national register of historic throws as the bridge's span is uniquely placed along the Indian Rock Disc Golf Course, one of two 18-hole disc golf courses at Rotary Park built by world champion and disc golf hall of famer, Johnny Sias. Go online at www.ghprd.org for more info.

East End Bridge/Gunner Gatski Bridge: Built in 1985 and designed by Arvid Grant of Washington, the East End bridge connecting Huntington and Proctorville, was only the second bridge of its kind in the U.S., as the 900-foot-high, cable-stayed bridge used concrete instead of steel in construction. View the bridge from the Guyandotte boat ramp as well as from the Adams Landing Marina just east of the bridge in Guyandotte. The bridge was renamed for Marshall University's first member of the Pro Football Hall of Fame, Frank "Gunner" Gatski in 2006.

Covered Bridge at Milton: The last of Cabell County's covered bridges, the Covered Bridge located at Milton's Pumpkin Park is the only example of a Howe truss bridge in the state. Originally built in 1875, the bridge was restored in 1971 and was brought to the Pumpkin Park (site of the famed WV Pumpkin Festival and the Cabell County Fair) in 2002. Enjoy a nice family walk in the paved trail that goes across the bridge and around a scenic pond. Go online at www.wvpumpkinpark.com for more info.

New River Gorge Bridge: Featured on the West Virginia state quarter, the world famous New River Gorge Bridge was built in 1977. The NRG Bridge is the second highest vehicle bridge in the U.S., at 876-feet-high, and at 3,030 feet in length, is the second largest single span steel arch in the Western Hemisphere. On the third Saturday in October, join tens of thousands of spectators and hundreds of BASE jumpers for the world's largest one-day extreme sports event, Bridge Day. Go online at www.officialbridgeday.com. For the brave in spirit, you can also take a year-round, Bridge Walk, a guided tour along the catwalk that sits about 850 above the New River, a nationally protected river. Go online at www.bridgewalk.com for more info.

Ashland's Twin Bridges: Painted UK blue, and green, respectively, the Ben Williamson Bridge and the parallel Simeon Willis Memorial Bridge connect Coal Grove, Ohio and Ashland, Ky. A great vantage point to see the bridges is Ashland's Veterans Riverfront Park that's received a $10 million makeover. Don't miss the Summer Motion festival at the park, located on the Ohio River, every July 4. The free festival is regularly named a Top 20 fest in the Southeast. Go online at https://www.facebook.com/SummerMotion for more info.

Kentucky

LAUREL GORGE

The calendar might have turned the page into November but thankfully somebody forgot to tell an Indian summer sun.

With a weekend that was hotter than a $10 Wii, and with soccer season finally in the rear-view mirror, we loaded up the ever-growing cookie crunchers to see if they could still hike their age or at least act it.

While there are a ton of great places to stomp the boots in the Tri-State, we chose a path less traveled for us and for many.

Located just south of Grayson Lake, along the beautiful Little Sandy River, is the 750-acre Ed Mabry/Laurel Gorge Wildlife Management Area.

An easy highway hop on I-64 and Ky. 7, the Laurel Gorge Cultural Heritage Center and its web of hiking trails are located along Laurel Curves Road at the juncture of Ky. 7 and the Old Route 32. It's about 40 minutes from Huntington.

You can park at the center, but armed with our GPS for some geocaching, we decided to take the scenic route. The short Homestead Trail leads from Route 7 and winds down below the new bridge and to the center, where you can access about three miles of interpretative trails that lead away from the noise of the traffic above and into the beautiful Gorge.

It only took a few steps along the extensive boardwalk (2/10 of a mile is completely accessible) for the rest of the family to understand why I had picked this place to hike.

Not unlike the New River Gorge and other parts of our region, Laurel Gorge is blessed with giant thickets of rhododendron that close in on the boardwalk that leads back into the Gorge and is

lined with good-sized Eastern hemlocks, tulip poplars, big leaf magnolias and towering rock walls.

Perfect for kids, the trail system has kiosks or info stations scattered about that concisely give good info on everything from tree and animal identification (like the fact that the only Eastern climbing salamander, the green salamander, hangs out here) to a wealth of info on the sheer rock cliffs pressed with everything from sandstone and white quartz pebbles to conglomerate.

Although we were lucky enough to get in on the last bits of fall color with the American beech still, almost greedily, hanging onto colored leaves, the Gorge, not unlike Lake Vesuvius and Carter Caves' Box Canyon and other rock-dominant trees, would make a wonderful winter hike.

While we walked all of the short trails, the favorite of the boys had to be the 1/2 mile Cliffline Trail that snakes around boulders and crevices below the towering sandstone cliffs that increasingly dripped with water on our way to a platform overlooking what is a waterfall in season flowing into Jason's Branch which flows into the Little Sandy River.

After walking off lunch, finding another one of the three geocaches in Laurel Gorge and combing through the creek, we made our way back to explore the Laurel Gorge Cultural Heritage Center.

The wildlife learning continues on the inside as the center, which has 28 interactive exhibits, hosts such unique and locally-made exhibits as a bird songs exhibit featuring audio recordings of bird songs matched with the wood carved bird species by the late Herman Peters.

Nestled into the cliffs, the center travels through time telling the stories of the Paleo Indians that first lived in Elliott County, through the pioneers, the moonshiners, and up to modern-day local musicians such as the Sloas Brothers, Keith Whitley and Don

Rigsby, as well as local artisans such as Minnie Adkins and Jimmy Lewis.

At the substantial exhibit paying tribute to Whitley, who racked up an amazing 19 singles and five straight No. 1 songs between 1984 to 1989 when the bluegrasser hit mainstream country, you can see many of his 45s including one of his first, "Turn to Love." It was cut with Patty Loveless. You can explore everything from scrapbooks of his shows and contracts to displays of his guitars and stage clothes.

While Eastern Kentucky has an abundance of well visited parks from Greenbo and Carter Caves to Grayson, Paintsville and Yatesville Lake, Laurel Gorge is an equally amazing place for hiking, and in season, canoeing on the beautiful, cliff-lined Little Sandy River that flows into and makes Grayson Lake.

Let's Go Trippin: Laurel Gorge

WHAT: Three miles of hiking trails at the 750-acre Ed Mabry-Laurel Gorge Wildlife Management Area.

WHERE: Laurel Gorge is located on Laurel Curves Road approximately three miles from Sandy Hook, Ky., in Elliott County.

HOW MUCH: Free.

HOURS: Hours at the center are 10 a.m. to 4 p.m. Monday through Friday, 10 a.m. to 5 p.m. Saturday and trail hours are dawn to dusk daily. Call 606-738-5543 for Sunday hours.

WHAT ELSE: The Laurel Gorge Cultural Heritage Center features 28 interactive exhibits on native wildlife, Appalachian life, Native Americans, country music history (Keith Whitley and Don Rigsby) and local artisans (Minnie Adkins, Jimmy Lewis and others).

GRAYSON LAKE: Just up the road from Laurel Gorge is Grayson Lake, the 1,512-acre lake has 74 miles of shoreline and is known for its amazing sheer sandstone cliffs. There's boat rentals at the Marina (606-474-4513), several trails including the 3-mile Lick Falls Trail camping and picnic areas.

GETTING THERE: From Huntington, take I-64 west to Grayson, Ky. Take Ky Route 7 south for approximately 23 miles. Watch for the signs to turn left into the Laurel Gorge.

STAYING THERE: The Little Sandy Lodge is nearby. Go online at www.littlesandylodge.com or call 606-738-5515.

There's camping from April 1 to Oct. 31 at Grayson Lake State Park. Go online at www.parks.ky.gov and click onto Grayson Lake.

EXPLORING THERE: Grayson couple Tim and Amanda Grigsby own and operate Grigsby Outdoor Adventures (http://grigsby.homestead.com/grigsbyoutdoors.html), and have scheduled paddle trips including ones of the Little Sandy River, Grayson Lake, Tygart's Creek, as well as spring, summer and fall campouts and customized roadtrips. They also offer a wide range of boating experiences including monthly guided moonlit paddles on the cliff-lined Grayson Lake, as well as drop-off and pick-up and rentals for folks to do self-guided day-trips on such scenic rivers as The Little Sandy (from the Grayson Lake spillway).

CONTACT: Go online at www.laurelgorge.com or call 606-738-5576

Some 'Rocking' Trails

Lake Vesuvius: The 8-mile Lakeshore Trail and 16-mile Backpacking Trails at Lake Vesuvius take hikers past a wealth of rock cliffs and scenic vistas around this lake in Lawrence County, Ohio and just north of Ironton. Park near the dam and picnic area to access the lakeshore loop. For more info, stop by the Ironton Ranger District, 6518 SR 93, Pedro, OH, call 740-534-6500 or go online at http://www.fs.usda.gov/recarea/wayne/recarea/?recid=6235

Raven Rock: Just west of Portsmouth is the Raven Rock State Nature Preserve. A steep, 500-foot climb takes up to a view from above the Ohio River valley, on a promontory of Mississippian age sandstone. According to folklore, Native Americans used the rock as a lookout. Weathering of the sandstone has resulted in three natural arches, the largest with a 10 foot span. The Naturalists at nearby Shawnee State Park, 4404 State Route 125, Portsmouth, Ohio, plans regular hiking trips to the top. Call 740-858-6652 or go online at http://naturepreserves.ohiodnr.gov/ravenrockarch

Hocking Hills State Park: Located near Logan, Ohio (between Columbus and Athens), Hocking Hills is famous for its waterfalls, caves and cliffs. Enjoy such off-season guided hikes as the annual Winter Hike at Hocking Hills every January, which celebrated its 50th year in 2015. Or stop by any other season for that six-mile trek from Old Man's Cave to Ash Cave. Go online at http://www.thehockinghills.org for more info.

Little Creek Park Trail Loop: Located at Little Creek Park in South Charleston. The Little Creek loop trail is only 1.5 miles and has a good pay-off with the impressive Devils Tea Table and views of Trace Fork creek. For more info, go online at http://cityofsouthcharleston.com/little-creek-park/

Beartown Rocks: Beartown State Park is small (only 107 acres) and far away from Huntington (in Pocahontas County about seven miles southwest of Hillsboro). But if you are in the neighborhood, say visiting Droop Mountain, then you will be blown away by the amazing short walk. Boardwalks connect through this almost bizarre natural collection of strewn boulders, cliffs and crags. The park is open daily from April to October. Go online at http://www.beartownstatepark.com/

Box Canyon Trail: Located at Carter Caves State Resort Park, 344 Caveland Dr., Olive Hill, Ky., Box Canyon is accessed at the

Cascade Cave State Nature Preserve. One of the most scenic trails at park, Box Canyon, while short (0.8 miles) is spectacular and perfect for families with smaller kids looking for a great but relatively easy hike (there is a hill up to the Canyon) that includes the Cascade natural bridge, the Box Canyon and the wind tunnel. There's also half a dozen more great loop trails at the park including the recommended Three Bridges Trail (three natural bridges in 3.5 miles), and the Four C's, a longer trail at just over seven miles. Call 606-286-4411 for more info.

Kentucky

WINTER ADVENTURE WEEKEND

Walking out of X Cave on Sunday morning, Brent Ray couldn't quit smiling and talking about the caves.

A veteran caver from Kenova, Ray got to spend the weekend with his family wild caving over in limestone-pocked Carter County, where he's been exploring the subterranean world for the past 30 years.

For the first time since 2008, and as part of the fourth annual Winter Adventure Weekend (in 2013), explorers were allowed to do wild caving at Carter Caves State Resort Park this past weekend.

More than 400 outdoors enthusiasts from six states took part in the weekend soaking up a buffet of outdoor adventures that included 140 different guided trips of such activities as: wild caving, horseback riding, tree climbing, canoeing, rock climbing, rappelling, ziplining, hiking, mountain biking, shooting and much more.

A 40-something who got hooked on wild caving when he was 11, Ray said getting to lead the Fern and Flood wild cave trips on Saturday as part of weekend, restored a piece that had been missing since the park's wild caving was outlawed in 2009 because of the threat of the epidemic bat disease White Nose Syndrome.

"The best way to describe it was like having a permanent grin on my face all weekend," Ray said of getting to cave again for the weekend. "It was a piece of me that was restored."

Ray, whose crew had to haul up a 16-foot-ladder for the Fern and Flood Caves trip, wasn't the only one who got in touch with his inner Tom Sawyer for some wild adventures.

Outdoors groups such as Ashland Cycling Enthusiasts and Kentucky State Parks shared into upstairs, downstairs at the lodge, folks tried to wriggle their way through the infamous Squeezebox.

The Saturday night timed Squeezebox finals competition saw reigning heavyweight champ and 2010 Marshall grad Jamie Dzierzak (Squeezebox winner 2005-08 and 2010-12) breeze to another win.

In the 176 to 200 pound Squeezebox competition, Boy Scout leader, Don Vartorella, 41, staved off competitors half his age with speed slides through the Squeezebox.

He got as low as 7 1/8 inches (in 27 seconds) and pulled and pushed his way through the box in as little as 4.3 seconds during the finals competition.

"My son Trent won it last year but he couldn't be here, he's stuck at college," Vartorella said. "It feels good to win it. It was like, 'Come on boys, keep up. I'm like three times your age. Come on, let's go.'"

While folks listened to adventure presentations during the day downstairs at the lodge, on Saturday night, the rooms were opened up for live music, as well as the auctions in which money was raised for the Friends of Carter Caves.

Throughout the weekend, a beehive of activity was found on the hill behind the lodge.

With set-up help by climber and longtime volunteer Brian Saul, Recreational Tree Climbing was in full swing Saturday afternoon as Scott Smith of Catlettsburg, Ky., and Jeff Rickman of Huntington helped people climb about 60 feet up into a towering black oak that sprawls majestically to about 100 feet high and in full view of the lodge dining room.

"Work those hips," Smith coached Bellevue, Ky., resident Patrick McCarthy, who came to climb the tree with his son, Sean McCarthy, 16. "Don't make your arms and upper body do all the work. Walk those legs up the tree."

Further down the hill from the lodge, some of the staff, made up of many expert climbers and rappellers who also participate in the annual Bridge Day rappel in West Virginia, set up a series of rope workshops including rock climbing, rope climbing, Down for Dummies (the rappel) and, the highline over near Smokey Bridge, the 90-foot-high natural bridge that lies down the hill between the lodge and the Smokey Valley Lake.

At Down for Dummies, expert rappellers Bruce Bannerman of Culloden and Julia Smith of Peebles, Ohio, harnessed up, then slowly walked and talked many nervous beginners off the cliff edge where they got to slowly drop 90-feet down a rope and see Kentucky's highest natural bridge.

"The cliff part was hard but just going down was easy," said a brave 9-year-old Sky Loomis, of Morehead, Ky.

While her 13-year-old daughter, Jenna only went down once, her mom, Julia Jones, of Morehead, Ky., hiked back up the hill for a second trip down after a breath-taking rappel into the heart of the bridge.

"It was awesome," Jones said. "I had walked that trail before but never saw it from that angle," Jones said.

Lakshmi Mahalingam, 23, of Hamilton, Ohio, said her group, the Tri-State Hiking Club, led by one of the main volunteers Andy Niekamp, put together the trip. She said she had to jump in for the adventures since it was only $30 for three day's worth of adventure trips.

"A lot of times you can get depressed in winter and don't want to go out so this is a great opportunity to get out and meet new people too," said Mahalingam, who did everything from rappelling to horseback riding and hiking.

Directly above Down for Dummies, a platform manned by such volunteers as Adam Wilson and Jerry Brandenburg, clipped in folks -- and even a few dogs -- to take a wild highline or zipline ride where they got a bird's eye view of Smokey Bridge.

Hollering for joy for most of her journey was Kentucky State Parks commissioner, Elaine Walker, who came over from Frankfort, to check out all the wonders of Winter Adventure Weekend.

From watching kids' faces as they made their way out of the Kenny McCoy Corrugated Cave and through the Squeezebox to seeing people of all ages climbing trees, hiking and ziplining, Walker said it was great to see so many people exploring the state park.

"What has got me is that people of all ages children and twentysomethings are everywhere and you don't see them tied to their iPhones or video games," Walker said. "They are outside, they are being physically active and that makes me so happy. This is what a park system is all about."

Let's Go Trippin: Winter Adventure

Winter Adventure Weekend: WAW at Carter Caves State Resort Park in Olive Hill., Ky., is like the ultimate back-stage pass to the caves of Carter County. It now has about 160 different trips, WAW has such caving trips as Sandy Cave Flotilla (where you lower a boat in a cave and float back into it), an overnight campout in Cascade Cavern, extreme crawling trips to caves on site like Bat Cave Back Door, and to Laurel, Rimstone and Horn Hollow. There's also trips to caves on private property as well including Tar Kiln Trek, The Tygart's Creek Regretta (a canoe and cave adventure). Go online at www.winteradventureweekend.com for more info.

Year-Round Walking Cave Trips at Carter Caves:
Cascade Cavern: There's two caves that are opened year round for guided walking tours. Those are Cascade Cavern, the largest of the more than 200 caves in Carter County. Cascade is a 75 minute-long tour that's about 3/4 of a mile long and that's easy save for 250 steps throughout the cave. Enjoy a 30-foot underground waterfall, the lake room, Cathedral Room and the dance hall where Kentucky musicians such as Heath and Molly still play music, and where the park hosts its Cave-In Movie series during the summer. Hours are cut back in the winter to Thursday through Sunday.

The other year around cave is X Cave, which is a shorter and easier trip that Cascade. (It takes about 45 minutes), X-Cave has two vertical joint passages that meander through a large layer of limestone, putting you up-close to beautiful cave formations like the Great Chandelier, the largest formation of stalactites in the cave, cave coral, and formations with such tell-tale names as the Giant Turkey, the Pipe Organ and Headache Rock.

Seasonal Caves: In addition to tours of Cascade and X-Cave, folks can also tour Bat Cave and Saltpetre Cave in the summer.

Saltpetre Cave was used during the War of 1812 as a source of the major ingredient in making gunpowder, Saltpetre, and is currently listed on the National Register of Historic Places. Tour is one-hour long and don't miss lantern tours as well offered several times a week. Tours available Memorial Day to Labor Day.

Bat Cave Walking Tour: The longest cave found within the park. The Bat Cave Walking Tour is a wild cave tour, so the trip is considered rugged and strenuous. The cave is completely undeveloped, it is not electrically lit, and there are no handrails or steps. Plan to get wet and muddy on this tour. You must pass a squeeze test before you go on this tour. You must be at least 6 years old and an adult must accompany those under 15 years old. Guardians will need to sign waivers for children under 18 yrs of age. Tour is two miles long and 2.5 hours. Helmets and flashlights are provided for the tour. Tours available Memorial Day – Labor Day.

Crawling Tours: Carter Caves has three crawling trips during the summer season:

Saltpetre Kid's Crawl: Tailor-made for kids 6-12 years old, the The Saltpetre Kid's Crawl is a great way to introduce your child to caving with a 1 1/2 hour trip. Kids will crawl on their hands and knees in small dark passages that will be lit only by the flashlight we provide. Parents are not permitted to accompany their children on the tour. Guardians will need to sign waivers for the children. Helmets and flashlights are provided for the tour. Tours available Memorial Day – Labor Day.

Bat Cave Crawling Tour: Three hours long, this cave trip (for those ages 12 and up), will have you crawling and walking through a lot of muddy and wet cave passages. Tours available Memorial Day through Labor Day.

Saltpetre Crawling Tour: Three hour long trip on both on the commercial routes of the cave and many of the wild unlit passages of the cave. You will be crawling both on your hands and knees and even doing some belly crawls through dry dusty passages during this tour. The cave is really cold, rocky and dusty. Tours Memorial Day through Labor Day.

More Places to Crave The Cave

Here's a look at a few more caves and cool underground places in the region.

Mammoth Caves: Located in western Kentucky near Bowling Green, Mammoth Cave National Park is one of the most visited NPS sites in the East. It's the world's longest caves system with more than 400 explored miles underground. Tons of cool trips are best taken off season (not in summer) when thick crowds gather and sell-outs are often. Go online at http://www.nps.gov/maca/index.htm for a full list of cave tours at Mammoth Cave.

Hidden River Cave/American Cave Museum: Located at 119 E. Main St., Horse Cave Ky., near Mammoth Cave, Hidden River was re-opeend in 1993 after being closed for 50 years because of groundwater pollution. The cave, which has been called "the greatest cave restoration success story in the United States" is now is filled with eyeless crawfish and other amazing cave critters. The cave museum with many wonders as well. For the adventurer, there's also the chance to try a 75-foot rappel into the mouth of a cave, as well as ziplines. Go online at www.hiddenrivercave.com

Lost River Cave: An hour-long underground boat tour at Lost River Cave at 2818 Nashville Road., in Bowling Green, Ky. It's Kentucky's only underground boat tour. Cost is $16.95 for those 12 and older. There's also a unique Kayak The Cave excursion for small groups (4 to 10) that's open year-round. There's also a Discovery Cave Crawl (cost is $25). For more info, go online at www.lostrivercave.com.

Smoke Hole Caverns: Located at 8290 N Fork Hwy Cabins, WV, (near Seneca Rocks), Smoke Hole Caverns has an easy, hour-long walking cave tour. Tours are year-round. Cost is $15 for adults. The grounds also features log cabins, a log motel, cottages, a gift shop, trout fishing and gem mining, Call 800-828-8478 or go online at www.smokehole.com.

Seneca Caverns: Located in Riverton, WV, eight miles south of Seneca Rocks on Route 33, Seneca Caverns features two show caves. Seneca Caverns has been open since 1928, and Stratosphere Cave, which is believed to be the state's oldest cave. It was re-opened in 2005. A guide will supply you with helmets and lights before you enter the cave for a one hour trip for those 13 and up. There's also wild caving trips for those ages 16 and up. Go online at www.senecacavernes.com for more info about Seneca Caverns which also includes gemstone mining, a restaurant, picnic areas and a gift shop.

Lost World Caverns; Located in Lewisburg, WV, Lost World Caverns was discovered in 1942 and is open year round for tours. A half mile loop takes you past such formations as the Snowy Chandelier, a 30-ton stalactite one of the largest in the U.S. There's four-hour-long wild caving tours as well. There's also a dinosaur museum at the cave where a prehistoric cave bear was discovered in 1967. Go online at www.lostworldcaverns.com for more info.

Greenbrier Bunker Tours: Located at the Greenbrier Resort. There are daily 90-minute tours for guests 10 years of age and older. See a one-of-a-kind Cold War construction began in 1958 as a safe house for the President and the top US government officials. The 112,544-square-foot bunker, built 720 feet into the hillside under The Greenbrier's West Virginia Wing. The Bunker has room for up to 1,100 people and was built with a power plant, water and fuel storage, a hospital, cafeteria, meeting rooms and decontamination chambers. Cost is $34 for adults and $17 for kids (ages 10 to 17). Go online at http://www.greenbrier.com/ Activities/The-Bunker/Bunker-Tours.aspx#sthash.bMltxKLf.dpuf

White Gravel Mines: Located at 4216 White Gravel Mcdaniel Road in Minford, Ohio, White Gravel Mines is an abandoned mine that hosts a handful of extreme events each year. Among those are paintball events in the mine, obstacle trail runs through the mud and the water-filled mine, and a Christian-themed Haunted House each fall called The Cavern of Choices that drew more than 1,600 people in two weekends in 2014. Call 740-776-0510 or go online at http://thewhitegravelmines.weebly.com/ for more info.

West Virginia

TIMBERTREK

With a long Labor Day weekend, Susan Coleman, of Hurricane, had just the cure for her teens.

Pack up Zach, 16, Jack, 12, and good friend Cora King, 15, and head over to Adventures on the Gorge for a wild day of playing, sliding, ziplining and climbing.

Described as "Swiss Family Robinson meets the Ewok Village," TimberTrek Aerial Adventure Park is fast becoming a popular attraction in the New River Gorge area.

Tucked into the tall tulip poplars and oak trees behind the back deck of the Rendezvous Lounge at AOTG, TimberTrek is a self-guided excursion along the unique system of 62 rope ladders, tightropes, giant nets, wobbly swinging bridges and zip lines that connect tree-based platforms that offer views of the forest canopy.

Set up with varying degrees of difficulty (fledging, beginner, intermediate and advanced) TimberTrek offers various color-marked routes (not unlike ski trails) that range from yellows and greens that are up to 15 feet off the ground to the intermediates and advanced (blue and then black diamond trails) that challenge Trekkers some 50 feet and more off the ground.

"We had done a mountain adventure like this last year in Vermont and I had heard about TimberTrek so we wanted to come try it," said Coleman.

While whitewater rafting and Adventures' TreeTops Canopy Tour and Gravity: New River Gorge Zip Lines, are still the main draw, Mike Carpenter, who manages TimberTrek for AOTG said the easily accessed aerial playground is increasingly becoming a big draw for families and youth groups visiting the Gorge.

"We had a family of seven the other day that let us know that they drove six hours to get here and they drove here 100 percent for this," Carpenter said. "It was one of those things they came here for this and then checked out some of our other activities while they were here."

Carpenter said one of the lures of TimberTrek, which is now in its second year, is that folks as young as 7 can get on it, while the zipline course is for kids at least 10 years old and at least 90 pounds, although ideally well over 100.

"This is something the young guys can do who might not be able to go on the river when it is a high flow or might not be able to go on the TreeTops because of the minimum weight, so they can do this for the younger guys and the older kids can do this as well."

To "do this" folks get into a climbing or ziplining harness, are given helmets and gloves and instructions on the double clipped carabiners and trolley that enable you to navigate the course safely without a guide.

Scattered throughout the course and on the ground, about half a dozen guides or "Trekkies" help in case anyone gets stuck or has a problem with an obstacle.

"I think people really like the fact that it is self guided and a big aspect of that is about self discovery," Carpenter said. "You don't have someone holding your hand the entire time. So they get to

look at an obstacle themselves and figure out the best way to do it, and there's no wrong way or right way -- just point A to point B. It is one of the few activities here at Adventures on the Gorge that is self guided."

Already laden with such nicknamed obstacles such as "Tommy

Knockers," "Greg's Element," "Stairway to Heaven," and "Satan's Sausages," the course is one that is best figured out in your own time and style, Carpenter said.

"Everything has its own unique twist and the key to it is just to take your time, and a lot of times just because somebody made it across in a certain way that doesn't mean it is the best way or that you have to do it that same way," he said. "Just take your time and take a look what you have to hold on to and step onto and decide for yourself and play to your strengths."

Letting people try to make their own way through the course provides a priceless boost to confidence levels of kids and adults who are afraid of heights, Carpenter said.

"Especially our younger guys seven or eight years old it is just a huge confidence builder for them, and adults also who may have heights issues, you get a huge sense of accomplishment after you finish that green or blue or even possibly that black."

Cora King, who was out on the course with the Coleman boys, said the course really made her face her fears and just go forward.

"It definitely tests your limits, your courage and your strength," she said of having to climb through the tunnels, Spidermanning your way through nets and climbing over tiny, swinging logs. "It was very fun, and I recommend everyone come and do it."

For those wanting to come do it, the prices are $79 for adults, $59 for youth, and there are group rates as well for the three-hour attraction.

And since the TimberTrek is within view of Buffler's BBQ Grill, Rendezvous Lounge on the Mill Creek campus (home to Songer and Rivermen rafting companies), spectators are always welcome to kick back, eat some 'cue and watch folks sliding, climbing, ziplining their way through the nearby canopy.

"That has been a great boost because one of the issues starting out was that it was kind of hard to market, so being right here in close proximity to where the rafting trip, ziplines and TreeTops meet up, people will always be over there and say, 'What is that thing?'" Carpenter said. "Then they will go over and watch some of our other guests climb and then they just want to get on it and see what it is all about."

Let's Go Trippin: TimberTrek

WHAT: TimberTrek Aerial Adventure Park is a fun, self-guided excursion along the unique system of 62 rope ladders, tightropes, giant nets, wobbly swinging bridges and zip lines that connect tree-based platforms that offer views of the forest canopy.

WHERE: Adventures On the Gorge, Ames Height Road in Lansing, W.Va., just north of the famous New River Gorge Bridge.

HOW MUCH: $79, $59 for youth and there are group rates as well for the three-hour attraction. They often run special deals as well.

WHEN: TimberTrek and TreeTops Canopy Tour will be open all winter with group minimums. Gravity will typically close after Thanksgiving if the weather is good enough to keep the road open.

WHO CAN GO? You must be at least 7 years old and not more than 260 pounds. Children under 14 must be supervised or accompanied by an adult.

HERE COMES THE NIGHT: All new is MoonTrek. That is TimberTrek at night in the dark and lit only by strings of holiday lights.

WHAT ELSE: Adventures on the Gorge is a world-class adventure vacation resort offering whitewater rafting, canopy tours, cabins, camping, fine dining and all-inclusive vacation packages that include everything from caving, rockclimbing and standup paddleboarding to TreeTops Canopy Tour, the Bridge Walk and Gravity: New River Gorge Zip Lines. On-site for families is such amenities as a playground, restaurants, a disc golf course and the Canyon Falls Swimming Hole, a 3,000 square foot pool with a 10,000 square-foot deck, and complete with waterfalls, stone work, a splash park and nearby snackbar.

ON THE WEB: Go online at www.adventurewestvirginia.com or www.adventuresonthegorge.com

Highlands Museum and Discovery Center: Located at 1620 Winchester Ave., in Ashland, the Highland Museum's Discovery Center is a paradise for the elementary school and pre-school set with such cool hands-on exhibits and play areas as Discovery Cavern, Treehouse of My Own, River Expedition, and recently renovated, The  Frank and Margaret Adkins Aviation Exhibit which features a model of one of the first planes, a quadruplane flown by Matthew Bacon Sellers in 1908 in Carter County, Ky. There's also the brand new Space Exhibit as well. Go online at http://highlandsmuseum.com for more info about the Museum which is open Wednesdays through Saturdays.

Ritter Park Playground: Named as one of the top 10 playgrounds in the U.S. by Architectural Digest when it was built decades ago, the Ritter Park natural play area is filled with sand and built of stone with natural tunnels and hiding places and a stone dinosaur. The new play are features a biplane swing, permanent steel congas, rock climbing structures all surrounded by a rim of willows. Go online at www.ghprd.org for more info on other cool playgrounds in the Greater Huntington Park and Recreation District including Harveytown Park (with a barn-themed playground), McClelland Park, April Dawn Park and Harris Riverfront Park in Huntington which has a playground and a new skatepark as well. Go online at ghprd.org

The Clay Center: The Clay Center's Avampato Discovery Museum houses two floors of hands-on science exhibits featuring more than 12,000 square feet of non-stop fun. Such award-winning interactive exhibits include Health Royale, Milton Gardner's Earth City, Myland Exploratory, Steamworks and Kidspace. There's special programs as well as the ElectricSky Theatre, a 61-foot-domed theater that hosts large-format educational films as well as planetarium shows with a star-ball filled with more than 10,000 stars. Go online at www.theclaycenter.org.

Heritage Farm Museum and Village: Located at 3350 Harvey Road, Huntington the national award-winning Heritage Farm features a petting zoo, the Hands-On Activity Center, an authentic 19th century One Room Schoolhouse, as well as a walk-through coal mine and such museums as the Progress of Appalachia Museum, American Transportation Museum and pioneer log cabin village. Special events include the monthly Way Back Weekends on the first Saturday or every month when the village comes alive with reenacts and artisans during this themed event. call 304-522-1244 or go online at http://www.heritagefarmmuseum.com/

Pump Up The Fun: Located at 6759 Merritts Creek Road, Huntington, Pump Up the Fun is a kids paradise with tons of inflatables for all ages. Seasonally, there's also a new inflatable water park. Call 304-733-2386 or go online at www.pumpupthefun.com.

Billy Bob's Wonderland: Located at 5 Cracker Barrel Drive, Barboursville, near the Huntington Mall, Billy Bob's has indoor laser tag, a video arcade and one of the last Rockafire Explosion animatronic bands playing hit songs for the kids. Outdoors, in season, there's putt putt golf and go-cart racing. Go online at www.billybobswv.com for more info.

COSI: Located in downtown Columbus, Ohio, at 333 W. Broad St., COSI has been named the No. 1 science center in the country by Parents magazine. Packed with more than 300 exhibits, COSI lets you explore distinct areas such as the space, Gadgets, Life, Progress, Ocean and WOSU, a working TV and radio station. In the Ocean exhibit, for parents with little kids don't miss the magical water-shooting splash area where Mighty Poseidon reigns over a mythical playground symbolizing the ancient stories of the sea. Go online at www.cosi.org for more info.

Cincinnati Museum Center at Union Terminal: Located in the art deco Union Terminal former railway station, the Cincinnati Museum Center features the Museum of Natural History and Science, an Omnimax Theater, The Cincinnati History Museum and, of course, The Duke Energy Children's Museum with such interactive areas as Kids Town, The Energy Zone, The Woods and Little Sprouts Farm. Go online at www.cincymuseum.org

West Virginia

POCAHONTAS COUNTY

While West Virginia may be small in area, we know how to stack, pack and pile things vertically

Like the cluttered Fred Flintstone closet and Chevy Chase's piled-high Vacation station wagon, there's plenty of things to find in the West Virginia mountains, it just takes a minute and a little work to get to them.

With a week off for Cabell County Spring Break, the Dave Trippin' crew loaded up the mini-van to the gills with ski gear, more Magic Makers discount costumes than should be legal, hiking boots, musical instruments, playing cards, magic tricks, and oh yes, the family hound, and headed over to do a little poking around Tucker and then Pocahontas Counties high in the West Virginia mountains.

While it takes a little more planning and prepping, we scoped out some pooch-friendly places and in West Virginia cabins a plenty can be found.

We started our trip over in Canaan Valley at what has become a grand family spring tradition and what is surely one of West Virginia's most unique spring break and end-of-ski-season festivals, the Snowy Luau, at the family-owned **Timberline Four Seasons Resort** (www.timberlineresort.com) that for the past 21 years has been bringing the irresistible mash-up of Hawaiian music, dance and pig roast with the wild and wonderful Snowy Luau slopeside traditions of snow sculpting, costume contests and fun and wacky on-the-slopes competitions.

While **Timberline Four Seasons Realty** (http://www.t4sr.com/) has plenty of pet friendly options for cabins, we needed to find a place for the rest of Spring Break week and scored a great deal at **Watoga State Park** south of Huntersville and Marlinton (304-799-4087 and www.watoga.com) where they were running a "Three Dog Night" deal through March 31 which folks could stay three nights (Sunday through Thursday) and receive a 50 percent discount. Toss in another $50 to have Milo, our Cheagle (Chihuahua/Beagle mix) and we had a solid place to bunk and explore the nearly endless wonders of one of West Virginia's largest counties.

Leaving Timberline on a Monday, we had an amazing drive over past Seneca Rocks and while we normally would have stopped and hiked and hit places like Seneca Caverns, we were full-throttle down WV 28 trying to get down to West Virginia's Space Place, Green Bank, W.Va.'s **National Radio Astronomy Observatory (NRAO)** that is only open 10 a.m. to 6 p.m. Thursday through Mondays before Memorial Day when it is then open daily from 8:30 a.m. to 7 p.m. with hourly tours from 9 a.m. to 6 p.m.

With only a handful of the guided van tours going out off-season we were questioning our timing when the receptionist took one look at our rugged crew and quickly handed us a walking tour map, told us we could take the dog on a free four-mile round-trip walking tour of the property, which saved us $20 (that the boys then quickly plowed back into the gift shop).

It is the rock star astrophysicist Neil deGrasse Tyson who says that "Everyone should have their mind blown once a day," and NRAO's excellent indoor Science Center and the trail that loops you around past 10 telescopes all constantly mapping, exploring and further defining our galaxy, does that and that and then some.

Although the van tour builds up to the Green Bank Telescope, we, out slogging through the field with a surround sound of gurgling stream and the hum of the GBT were drawn magnetically to the GBT that at 485 feet tall is bigger than Egypt's Great Pyramid (450 feet) and dwarfing the Statue of Liberty (305 feet).

While the GBT has helped produce images of the surface of Venus, has detected three new pulsars,and has helped generate a detailed image of the Orion Nebula (hey nice rhinestone belt there Orion), we were also equally impressed with the greatest hits so to speak of the smaller working telescopes along the way.

Nearly back to the Science Center we were surprised to see one satellite start moving when we walked by (Did it detect aliens (middle schoolers) in its presence?

I guess not, we stopped and were enthralled by the U.S. Naval Observatory's 20-meter telescope (the fastest telescope on site) can rock two degrees per second and completely go to an opposite position in 90 seconds. We found out this was the telescope that measures the Earth's orientation, rotation and motions of the continent, and detected that Earth slows down in El Nino years.

With our minds effectively blown (even on a Spring Break Monday), we decided to leave the GBT to its job of detecting cosmic clues, as the Dave Trippin' crew headed off to go explore more of the expansive Pocahontas County, which at 942 square miles is the third largest county in West Virginia.

Known as the birthplace of river as Pocahontas County is the site of the headwaters for eight rivers: Cherry River, Cranberry River, Elk River, Gauley River, Greenbrier River, Tygart Valley River, Williams River, and Shavers Fork of the Cheat River, the area is best known as a warmer seasonal destination for fishing, biking and hiking.

For a modern family in much need of a forced "unplugged" session we arrived just a wee bit early in the late days of winter but in some ways it was right in time since we ran into no crowds and no cell service.

With still inches of snow on the hills and trails we found

Watoga (which has 10 year-round cabins) practically empty and with no cell service, ended up with some solid fam time at the cabin - teaching the kids to play Euchre, playing with the dog, looking at the stars nightly, going on hikes, building lots of fireplace fires, playing in the creek and even fishing with dental floss (more on that later).

Accurately touted as "Nature's Mountain Playground," Pocahontas is packed with must-see stops for the fam. You can't do it all in three days but we tried.

With many places such as Cass still closed for the season, we laced up the hiking boots and with Will's "Guardians of the Galaxy," soundtrack blasting we headed out for what Pocahontas County CVB calls its "Wonders and Waterfalls" tour which was broken into two days of themed exploring such places as Beartown State Park, Droop Mountain, Cranberry Glades and Falls of Hills Creek, all of which we checked out.

Although we had to punt trips to Pretty Penny Cafe (a popular

live music spot in Hillsboro on the weekends) and the Pearl Buck homeplaces (both closed), we over the course of a couple days made slippery tracks at a handful of amazing places that were "bearly" open since most places had few if any human tracks but some rather large clawed prints through the snow causing us all to pause and pray black bears do not prefer pasty white meat.

A must-stop is the **Falls of Hills Creek,** which by the time you get their dear reader will not require practically an ice pick and crampons to access the bottom.

Located on the **Highland Scenic Highway (WV 39/55)** the Falls trailhead is located five miles west of Cranberry Mountain

Visitor Center and the trail winds you down into a gorge to three falls (25, 45 and 63 feet), the last being the second highest waterfall in the state next to the famed Blackwater Falls.

We were at the falls on St. Patrick's Day alone in a world still coated in white, the only green, the hearty Giant Rhododendruns whose green umbrella-like leaves were still folded in shuddering from the last of winter's cold but the waterfall roaring in its full glory of snowmelt.

For waterfall freaks, you can read more these falls and others in Kevin Adams book, "Waterfalls of Virginia and West Virginia," and they are also featured in the Monongahela National Forest Hiking Guide by West Virginia Highlands Conservancy (a book I highly recommend for folks exploring the West Virginia mountains and the 900,000-acre Mon).

While we unsuccessfully tried to take the untreated, unplowed and impassable with our minivan, Highland Scenic Highway up to Marlinton, it's highly recommended in season, as the only U.S. Forest Service managed parkway in the States, is packed with 14 scenic stops that include scenic overlooks and scenic trails.

We popped down on U.S. 219 to roll into Marlinton home to such lunch spots as **Rayetta's Lunch Box (304-799-4888)** and the

Greenbrier Grille and Lodge (304-799-7233) which has a restaurant, five rooms with private baths, and perhaps most important in these parts, Wi-Fi Internet access.

While the fam decided against sitting on the deck overlooking the Greenbrier River on the brisk afternoon, we had a ball watching some toddlers enjoying what the Grille is somewhat famous for, the feeding of the quite spoiled local duck population lapping up pellets from the river below.

The Grille also happens to be across the street from a simply stunning mural "Over Bonnie," by Pocahontas County artist Molly Must that pays tribute to the West Virginia poet laureate Louise McNeill, who passed away in 1993. The mural also pays homage to her father and fellow writer G. D. McNeill who was best known for his short stories about the forests of Pocahontas County.

As luck would have it (wow, I really did pack everything), I put the "Guardians of the Galaxy" soundtrack on pause, and popped in the quite appropriate new WV audio poetry CD, **"My People Was Music"**

Backed by the world famous Bing Brothers string band, WV poet Kirk Judd waxes poetic on the magnificent sights of Pocahontas County and its inspiring people like the late, great poet Louise McNeill, and to be able to listen to such incredible poems that are so set in that place like "Cold Run," "On Cranberry," "The Ground of Eden," "For Louise McNeill," and "Beware!Meat Eating Plants Surround You," was a real and rare treat for all of us. With Judd's poems echoing in our ears we headed back into the mountains that afternoon to explore one of WV's smallest but most unique state parks, **Beartown Rocks State Park (304-653-4254, www.beartownstatepark.com)**.

Since our oldest son Jake and I had been here two years ago while accompanying Mike Sheets and his Western Virginia Military Academy (the Huntington Middle School Civil War reenacting unit), we were stoked for Toril and Will to breathe in the bizarre wonder of Beartown, the 107-acre park known for its unusual sandstone rock formations.

Taking the boardwalk you wind through, below, beside and above this jaw-dropping assemblage of rocks and boulders.

Interestingly, one of the first things I noticed on this quiet return trip in winter was a weathered plaque tucked into the woods at the entrance that explains Beartown's unique tie to Huntington as the land was purchased in 1970 with funds from the Nature Conservancy and a donation from Mrs. Edwin G. Polan, in memory of her son, Ronald Keith Neal, who lost his life in the Vietnam War.

With the afternoon sun gaining strength and sending the temperatures into the 60s and our spirits soaring, we drove back from Beartown located on the eastern summit of Droop Mountain to the **Droop Mountain Battlefield State Park** (www.droopmountainbattlefield.com and 304-653-4254)

Although some of the park's roads were closed, the ranger said we could hike out to the unique log-stacked Lookout Tower, built by the men of the Civilian Conservation Corps in 1935.

After climbing to the top of the tower, we wound up taking our dog's lead. Milo stretched out on the scrubby grass field with that amazing panoramic view, his eyes drooped and he sat and soaked up the sun.

Who can argue with that. One by one, we were laid out in the grass watching the wispy cirrus cloud spirits and characters that formed and faded away across the blue sky.

After the hike heavy Tuesday, we decided Wednesday to soak in the quiet goodness of Watoga spending the morning relaxing and then in early afternoon heading out just down the road from our cabin to hike the famed 400-acre **Brooks Memorial Arboretum** at Watoga State Park in Pocahontas County.

The Arboretum, named for noted WV naturalist Fred E. Brooks, was dedicated in 1938, and was one of the first of its kind in West Virginia and one of the first at a state park in the United States.

While the Arboretum has 6.5 miles of trails with many trees, shrubs and other plants labeled along the way, we traced the Dragon's Draft Trail back into the Brooks before the trudging and crisscrossing of the creeks caused us to retreat.

Since we had passed several fisherman angling for some of those stocked trout in Watoga's 11-acre lake that was mostly iced out, me and the boys caught the fishing bug.

Bad for us, since we had started this Spring Break trip at a ski resort, none of us, who've got multiple rods and even a Pocket Fisherman for goodness sakes, had packed any fishing gear.

But I couldn't deny the boys a Spring Break fishing trip and thus we foraged like the Boy Scouts we are in the mega van of junk and unearthed the trout spinner I had bought over at Harper's General Store, and about four yards of dental floss.

Tossing the uh fishing gear into the backpack with some snacks we headed out for what ended up being a glorious afternoon hanging out amongst the shoreline Giant Rhododendruns. Will and Jake whittled, they took turn casting the dental floss on a stick fishing rod and hopefully learned a lesson that doesn't take a

$50,000 bass boat to teach - that a bad day of fishing is better than a good day at the office.

Rolling out Thursday morning, it was Cranberry Glades or Bust and with the more than mile-long entryway to the boardwalk still packed with a half foot of ice and snow, we parked and hoofed it to get a winter view of the 750-acre Cranberry Glades Botanical Area, one of the largest area of bogs in West Virginia.

While we were months away from getting to see rare beauties like the snake mouth orchids, we did get to see the red foliaged meat-eating pitcher plants as well as some reindeer lichens in this "southern refuge for northern plants."

Back out on U.S. 219 and rolling south through Lewisburg to make the 3 1/2 westward drive home, the radio station 88.5-FM fired up the old bluegrass song, "Wild Mountain Honey," which seemed like the perfect song to sum up the trip.

Although we didn't get to soak in some of the mountains' main attractions like the Glades or the Greenbrier River Trail in the height of their wonder, we did get a sweet and savory foretaste of mountain glory.

And during a frosty Spring Break what more could you ask for.

Let's Go Trippin: Pocahontas County

Here's a closer look few things to do over in the mountains of Pocahontas County, Wet Virginia

WHAT TO SEE: Touted as "Nature's Mountain Playground," Pocahontas County is packed with must-see stops including Cranberry Glades Botanical Area, Cranberry Wildness Area, Falls of Hills Creek, Highland Scenic Highway, Beartown State Park, Droop Mountain Battlefield State Park, Watoga State Park, Cass Scenic Railroad, the Durbin and Greenbrier Valley Railroad, the National Radio Astronomy Observatory, Snow shoe Mountain, the Pocahontas County Opera House, the Greenbrier River Trail, the West Fork Trail and the Pearl S. Buck Birthplace Museum.

SCENIC DRIVE: Try the Highland Scenic Highway Parkway (WV150) a 45-mile route from Richwood to U.S. 219 on Elk Mountain, north of Marlinton. There's more than a dozen featured points of interest including many overlooks here in the heart of the Monongahela National Forest.

WHAT TO LISTEN TO: Backed by The Bing Brothers string band, Kirk Judd waxes poetic on the magnificent sites of Pocahontas County and its inspiring people like the late, great poet Louise McNeill in his new audio poetry CD and book, "My People was Music" ($25/Mountain State Press, www.mountainstatepress.org).

ON THE WAY: If you roll 39/55 don't miss a stop in Richwood, famous for its spring time Feast of the Ransom, ramp dinner. If you go through Greenbrier County, don't miss a stop by Lewisburg, which was named America's favorite small town by Travel and Leisure Magazine. go online at www.downtownlewisburg.com. And just a short piece from Lewisburg is White Sulphur Springs home to the world famous Greenbrier Resort, home to the famous Underground Bunker tour, the home of the New Orleans Saints summer camp, the Greenbrier Classic PGA golf tournament and more. Go online at www.thegreenbrier.com for more info.

ON THE WEB: Online at www.naturesmountainplayground.com for more info on things in Pocahontas County or call 800-336-7009.

ALL QUIET ON THE MOUNTAIN FRONT: Because of the Green Bank, West Virginia-based National Radio Astronomy Observatory, there is a 13,000 square mile National Radio Quiet Zone where there's zero cell service. Call 800-336-7009 to find the limited areas where it is available. Many businesses and libraries in central and southern parts of Pocahontas County offer free Wi-Fi as well.

PET-FRIENDLY CABINS IN POCAHONTAS COUNTY: Watoga State Park (800-225-5982) and Pocahontas Cabins (614-834-9811). Also most all camping in the area is pet-friendly as well.

OTHER PLACES IN WEST VIRGINIA TO STAY WITH YOUR POOCH: West Virginia State Parks has 17 state park and forest that are pet-friendly. Some of the closest ones with some pet friendly cabins are Beech Fork State Park and Cabwaylingo State Forest. Some of the most popular includes places such has Cass, Babcock, Watoga, Blackwater Falls and Pipestem. Read more at www.wvstateparks.com/pet-policy.htm.

Other cool science centers

Clay Center for the Arts and Sciences of West Virginia: Located in downtown Charleston, W.Va., The Clay Center's Avampato Discovery Museum houses two floors and more than 12,000 square feet of interactive fun with such award-winning exhibits like Health Royal, Kidspace, Milton Gardner's Earth City, Mylan Explore-atory, STEAMworks. There's also a recently

renovated Digital Dome and the ElectricSky theater which shows large-format film. Call 304-561-3570.

Highlands Museum and Discovery Center: (Shown in the above photo) is located at 1620 Winchester Avenue in downtown Ashland, Ky. The Highlands Museum is a blend of history as well as a hands-on science center. Downstairs in the Discovery Center, check out the new space science exhibition hall. Located in the Discovery Center, it houses the new exhibit "Satellites, Aerospace & the Bluegrass State."

This exhibit, designed by Morehead State University's Space Science Program will inform visitors about the roles satellites play in the field of aerospace and highlight Morehead State University's role in preparing students to work in the challenging field of aerospace. Call 606-329-8888 or go online at www.highlandsmuseum.com

for more info.

COSI: Located at 333 W. Broad St., in downtown Columbus, Ohio, COSI (the Center for Science and Industry) is one of the largest science centers in the Midwest, with tons of classic interactive exhibits. Ride COSI's High Wire Unicycle two stories up, drive a Mars rovers in space and much more at COSI, which has 320,000-square-feet of floor space, plus ten major exhibition areas. Dive into the depths of the seas in Ocean. Time-travel in Progress. Experience the wonders of our Universe through a Giant Screen film. Go online at www.cosi.org or call 614-228-2674 for more information.

Cincinnati Museum Center: Located in the gorgeous and historic Union Terminal at 1301 Western Ave., Cincinnati, the Cincinnati Museum Center is home to a bunch of museums including the Museum of Natural History and Science. Inside see such unique exhibits as The Cave, the Ice Age, a Memorial exhibit to Ohio astronaut Neil Armstrong (the first man to walk on the moon), a STEM Discovery Lab, a Dinosaur Gallery and more. For more info, go online at www.cincymuseum.org or call 513-287-7000.

West Virginia

CAMDEN PARK'S HAUNTED HOUSE

Somewhere soon after testing your second grade driving mettle at Safety Town, a next badge of courage must be earned by Huntington area youth.

You must go to the sign of the happy clown, you must enter, you must walk up to Camden Park's Haunted House, and you must put your sweaty hands on the cold steel bar as a ride operator shoves the car around the corner and into the darkness.

That time-tested youth-courage builder known as the Haunted House, is just one of 20 rides and attractions that are drawing in folks every October weekend as Camden Park continues Spooktacular that runs 6 to 11 p.m. every Friday and Saturday in October.

The Halloween-themed event, which celebrates its 17th year in 2015, features the Haunted Train Ride, complete with animatronics, special effects, costumed characters and a graveyard full of zombies; the new "Labyrinth de Mort" a special horror filled walk-through maze, and a complete restoration of the park's historic Haunted House by Connecticut dark house artist Chuck Burnham.

Burnham, who has painted some 100 fun houses and dark houses all over the country, said it was a dream come true to get to paint and restore Camden Park's Haunted House, as it is the oldest remaining dark ride designed and painted by the late, legendary artist Bill Tracy.

Burnham, who worked as an apprentice for dark house artist Peter Rasulo for more than 20 years, said he wanted to capture those original colors and shock and awe of the original Tracy Haunted House that was installed in the spring of 1961 at the park.

Working with local artist Chuck Wheeler, who did the sounds,

lighting and graphic car wraps for the Haunted House re-do, B
urnham said they took out the "updated" elements of the eight-
turn ride, and went back to the original recipe, some of that
delicious darkness of the 1960s.

"You talk to any of your older uncles and they'll say those old
dark rides were better," Burnham said. "It was the element of
surprise."

Burnham, who is 38 and grew up fascinated with dark rides and
artists on such albums as KISS and Meatloaf, said they ran 100 cars
through the Haunted House before figuring out exactly where to
do the tricks.

"It's got to be by the split second that psychology of how to
make the painting and the sculpturing work," Burnham said. "In
my industry they say I've got an old wrist. I'm 38 but it looks like
I've been doing this longer than I've been alive. The thing that
brought out Bill's work was how he could make the smallest
amount of trim so bright. He really colored everything kind of
dark and he wanted you to look at what he made and have it stand
out."

Jack Boylin, who owns and operates the family-owned theme
park, said the park feels lucky to have tracked down Burnham,
whose restoration of the historic house has made it better than
ever.

Boylin said they were looking into redoing the Haunted House,
but by happenstance found one of the country's best old-school

dark house painters.

"We had the basic model and he's made it into a deluxe Bill Tracy model," Boylin said of Burnham's homage to Tracy, who passed away in the 1970s.

Boylin said when he began working at his family's park in 1995, that only one Bill Tracy element remained inside, and that Plexiglas had been added on many of the turns to protect the various skeletons and ghouls that spring out.

Experts say Camden Park and area residents are lucky to have such an amazing part of the past.

While there were once hundreds of dark rides spooking kids and adults at amusement parks around the country, only a handful of these antique rides remain.

In fact, Camden Park's Haunted House is one of only two gravity-fed Pretzel rides still left in the United States, according to George LaCross, editor of Laff in the Dark, a Web site dedicated to dark rides and funhouses.

Myrtle Beach's Haunted Hotel is gone, ditto for Phantasmagoria out in Oklahoma, the FrightZone in Pennsylvania, Whacky Shack in Witchita, and so is even Dante's Inferno at Coney Island's Astroland that was closed in 2008.

A favorite ride of Jack Boylin, the third generation of Boylins to operate Camden Park, the Haunted House was originally a Laff In The Dark ride that was called the Laughing Lady.

He also believes it was re-themed in the '60s. However, he doesn't know much more than that since the oldest employee at the park, which opened in 1903, only goes back to 1980.

LaCross said the House was most likely upgraded to a double-decker gravity ride in the 1960s when there were a lot of carnivals that used that style of ride.

"They were perfect for disassembly but there were some permanent installations," LaCross said. "There used to be a similar one at Seaside Heights in New Jersey that was also called the Haunted House."

The other gravity Pretzel ride that remains is the Devil's Den at Conneaut Lake, a historic amusement park in western Pennsylvania, LaCross said.

"Basically what transpires is the chain brings a light-weight Pretzel car up and from there the gravity feeds the ride as the upstairs floor is pitched in a way that it goes by gravity over a balcony and then drops like a roller coaster," LaCross said. "Some people confuse this with a roller coaster, but it is a dark ride. It uses the same mechanics as a roller coaster but was intended to be a portable, low-maintenance type of ride without an electrified track."

LaCross said that although they are not for sure when the Haunted House was installed at Camden Park, they do know that the very similar Devil's Den went into Conneaut in 1968.

From his research, LaCross also knows that Bill Tracy, who didn't work for Pretzel, but who did a lot of facade work, designed the facade at Camden Park and the nearly identical Haunted House at Seaside Heights in Jersey.

LaCross figures what happened at Camden Park was that a single-rail Pretzel ride was installed at in the 1940s and that in the 1960s, the park upgraded to the gravity-fed double decker.

"It clearly is a Pretzel anywhere from say 1940 to 1960," La Cross said. "A lot of people had them installed in the 1930s but they really started taking off after that. Really right up to the 1970s everyone had one, but little by little they started disappearing. I don't think anyone would ever tell you it was because of a lack of interest in riders."

Boylin said the Haunted House is still one of the most popular rides at the park, and is tricked out especially for Spooktacular with a fog rising from the rails and new creatures to pop out once you're inside.

The pre-cursor to larger roller coaster rides such as Blazing

Fury at Dollywood, the dark rides revel in the jolt of surprise.

"It is the excitement of the unknown because you really don't know what is inside of these things," LaCross said. "You really don't know what lies ahead and it takes several rides before you get the lay of the land, so you get a lot of repeat riders, and it's tough to remember what you've just seen the first time through."

Early in their history, dark houses didn't have spooky facades.

"Especially those in the late 1920s and 1930s just simply said Pretzel and had questions marks on the facade making people wonder what they were getting themselves into."

The Pretzel Ride company, a Bridgeton, N.J.-based company that patented the dark ride in 1928, went out of business in 1978.

Like Camden Park, which has tricked out the ride for Halloween and made upgrades to what's inside, LaCross said some of the other surviving historic dark rides have taken advantage of new technology with electronic figures and the use of digital sound as well.

LaCross said he feels there should always be a spot for the dark ride at family amusement parks.

"I've spoken to a lot of roller coaster people and they've reached a point now that they can't build these things any higher or faster because people just can't sustain it physically," LaCross said. "So, I think there too are a lot of people who don't ride roller coasters, who may be afraid of heights or have motion sickness and for them the dark ride is a great alternative to that. It's something fun they can ride."

LaCross has an online petition drive called Save The Rails to try and save Playland's Zombie Castle and Flying Witch from being torn down later this year in Rye, New York.

LaCross said park-goers in West Virginia are very lucky to have a family-owned park with such a bevy of historic rides including The Whip, the Train and, of course, the Haunted House.

"If it's in the hands of somebody with a legacy involved, I can't tell you how lucky you are," He said. "It is like the amusement park is an appendage. It is part of them and to sell it or neglect it would be like an act against their own family. If they're holding onto it and putting money back into it, it becomes a community center with community functions there. That is the way things used to be decades ago, but it is rare today. People in West Virginia should really appreciate that and not take it for granted. I have had the rug pulled out from me twice, and once those parks are gone, they are gone. There are memories, but it still hurts."

Let's Go Trippin: Camden Park

WHAT: West Virginia's only amusement park, Camden Park in operation since 1903.

WHERE: Five miles west of downtown Huntington along U.S. 60 West at 5000 Waverly Road, Huntington.

WHEN: Open May through October each year. Spooktacular is open Fridays and Saturdays in October.

WHAT'S THERE: A host of historic rides such as the Mangel's-built Whip and Mini-Whip, the Lil' Dipper and Big Dipper wooden roller coasters, the carousel, Log Flume and The Train. Also a blend of family-friendly newer rides such as the Kite Flier, the Flying Scooters, The Rattler and such attractions as the 18-hole West Virginia Adventure mini-golf and the Swan Lake Paddleboats.

PARK HISTORY: The park is owned and operated by the Boylin family. Jack Boylin's grandfather, J.P.. transformed the park in the 1950s from a trolley line picnic park to an amusement park that through the years has had a roller rink, a zoo, a paddlewheel boat, and tons of national acts such as Garth Brooks, and Vince Gill play the park.

CONTACT: Visit www.camdenpark.com, call 304-429-4321.

Guyandotte Ghosts Haunted and Historic Walking Tours: Since 2008, they have hosted walking tour of historic Guyandotte. Haunted tours run on weekends before Halloween as well as during the annual Guyandotte Civil War Days, an annual event that will mark the 154th anniversary of the Civil War Raid on Guyandotte in 2015. This tour is a mile walk through the historic section of Guyandotte (in Huntington) with lantern-swinging costumed characters spinning tales of true history, weird lore and tales. Go online at http://guyandotteghosts.com/ for more info.

Fallsburg FearPlex: A haunted attraction that features five attractions at 5877 Kentucky 3., outside of Louisa, Ky. Fearplex saw 17,000 customers in 2013. They started in 1987 with the Fallsburg Haunted House, expanded in 2012 with Hell's Wagon Paintball. In 2013, they added a third attraction, Crazy Creek. For the 2014 season, they added Appalachian Nightmare 3D, a 3D blacklight complete with live actors, and Backwoods Blackout, a pitch black maze in the same building as Appalachian Nightmare 3D. Call 606-686-3030. They are also on Twitter and Instagram, both @FHHFEARPLEX.

Spooktacular' Cave-in Movies: Carter Caves State Resort Park in Olive, Hill, Ky., hosts monthly Cave-In Movies, including a family-friendly spooky film each October before Halloween. Admission is $5 and seating is not provided, so it is BYOC (bring your own chairs) Concessions are available.Tickets are sold at Cascade Cave. Call 606-286-4411.

Ric Griffith's Pumpkin House: Kenova, W.Va. mayor Ric Griffith's historic home at 748 Beech St., gets turned into a jack o' lantern wonderland each Halloween. Griffith directs community volunteers who carve about 3,000 pumpkins that are lit for a one-of-a-kind display. Enjoy the pumpkin symphony with lights coordinated to music, and events at the C-K Autumn Fest that coincides with the lighting. Go online at www.ckautumnfest.com for more info.

Haunted Tunnel: Located at the junction of Ohio 93 and U.S. 52, the Haunted Tunnel has been operated by the Ironton's Lion's Club since 1992. The Haunted Tunnel takes place every Friday and Saturday in October. All proceeds go to Lions Club charities.

Halloweast: Located in Charleston's East End, Halloweast features a week of themed Halloween events including a horror-themed art show, (ArtMares), a murder mystery, a zombie walk, a zombie 5K, and a HallowEast costumed pub crawl among other things. Go online at www.halloweast.com for more info.

Haunted Maze: The Maze at Cooper Farms in Milton, located behind the old Milton Middle School, hosts a haunted maze called The Field of Screams through its seven-acre corn maze. Go online at http://www.cooperfamilyfarms.net/ to find out more about the Field of Screams and the Farms' new biplane course.

Mothman Bus Tours: The Mothman Museum hosts regular and narrated bus tours through the TNT area (where Mothman was spotted), walk the trails and get admission to the museum, a certificate and bumper sticker. Admission is $19.95 and $14.95 for kids (12 and under). Go online at www.mothmanmuseum.com for more info.

Whipple Ghost Hunts: Fridays and Saturdays in October: Whipple Company Store Ghost Tours, Scarbro, W.Va., in the heart of the New River Gorge. On this ghost hunt inside the 100-year-old building, explore unexplainable sights and sounds as you visit the ballroom, the walk-in safe, the hidden floor, the embalming room and the basement. Ages 21 and up. Call 304-465-0331; or go online at www.whipplecompanystore.com

Weston Haunted House at Trans-Allegheny: The annual haunted house at the famous Trans-Allegheny Lunatic Asylum, 71 Asylum Drive, in Weston. A frightening live haunted attraction held from dark until midnight at the asylum that's perennially in the top 10 haunted attractions in the U.S. The largest hand-cut stone masonry building in North America, was birthed in the Civil War. Built to house 250 people it reached its peak in the 1950s fwith 2,400 patients in overcrowded and generally poor conditions. Closed in 1994, the former mental hospital hosts a bevy of events including The Asylum Ball, plays, zombie Paintball, historic tours and the haunted house. Go online at http://trans-alleghenylunaticasylum.com/ for more info

West Virginia

SNOWY LUAU

What a short, strange trip this winter has been.

With no snow here in Huntington, our boys and the little neighbor twins had taken to the hobby of "mud-boarding" — taking turns riding snowboards and war-whooping down our snowless steep hill stripping practically every blade of grass within a country mile.

So before our hill became as shaved as Howie Mandel's head, we packed up the Lavender boys and headed out in this odd space between winter and spring to search for the last slivers of snow and the first signs of ramps — both the eating and the terrain park kind.

We found both species of ramps high in the Allegheny Mountains over in Canaan Valley, the highest valley east of the Mississippi, where we hunkered down in a cabin aptly titled "Abundant Blessings" at **Timberline Four Seasons Resort** (1-800-SNOWING) for a few days of much-needed Dave Trippin.'

Back in the Tri-State now for almost a dozen years, I appreciate more and more what Larry Groce told me when we first moved back — that the Mountain State has the lowest BS factor of about any state he's been to, and that the best stuff in the WV isn't usually found on a billboard.

That combo of a laid-back but an amazing time without a crushing crowd of people was certainly found over in Canaan Valley, a great mountain getaway for any season as its completely surrounded by sweet day-tripping spots such as Canaan Valley National Wildlife Refuge, Blackwater Falls and Canaan Valley State Parks, Dolly Sods Wilderness Area, Seneca Rocks, and, of course, the brewpub and cool restaurant-packed mountain towns of Davis and Thomas.

With broiling unseasonable temps in the upper '70s, and a mountain of snow up at Timberline melting by the minute, we made fast tracks over to 18th annual Snowy Luau, the annual tropics-filled festival to hit those slopes like a flour-bomb on Kim Kardashian.

This was the second time we'd been over for the Snowy Luau and I hope we can make it an annual tradition as the mountain is packed with all kinds of coolness — not the least of which is skiing in attire that makes you looks like you just joined Jimmy Buffett's Coral Reefer Band.

A real Hawaiian band, the Hoaloha Polynesian Review, rolls over from Washington, D.C., armed with all the ukuleles, drums and hulu dancers that can fit into a van. Those folks played tunes throughout the weekend as all the cool kids in school like veteran H-town skater and snowboarder Tim Cline (dressed in a Cincinnati Bengals meets grass skirt costume) were seen sliding down the mountains in such contests as the costume parade that also featured a minotaur and a Cookie Monster. For the record, Cliney bested Cookie Monster and friends for second place — a $15 tab at Timbers Pub.

Add the outdoor smoked pig, and the night-time spectacle of a super-sized bonfire, the lava flow down the mountain (skiers with torches) and then fireworks on top of the mountain and you have a winter-ending festivus that is truly a refreshingly odd slice of Mountain State life.

Not unlike hitting the last day of Gauley River season in the fall, I have come to love these waning weekends in the outdoors as you run into the folks who are there for the love of doing it — and in this case getting in one more run on the slopes as the creeks in nearby Dolly Sods Wilderness Area were roaring with water coming off the melting mountains of snow.

I met Amy Benefield and John Huff, two ski instructors at Ober Gatlinburg, where they had only 52 skiable days this season, up for the sixth year to enjoy skiing in the West Virginia mountains. Ober had closed on her birthday, but by golly they were going to get a ski on somewhere.

Out on the snow, I was energized meeting such folks who, as Buffett said have "grown older but not up" like Elkins resident Kevin Lynch, a recent Fairmont State grad who was putting his degree to work frantically trying to beat some tweeners who had built a Pepsi-spewing snow volcano in the snow sculpting contest. For the record, Lynch's Great White Shark carved out of a snow pile was good enough for second place.

While most ski trips are weekend blasts, we had the cabin for a couple extra days because of Spring Break, and blame it on the wild-mountain-spirit of fresh-dug ramps in Timberline's Ramp Meatloaf and Ramp Burgers and Hellbender Burritos' Ramp Quesadilla, but our posse was burning with the call of the wild.

With both a biologist and a baby on board in our crew, I knew we needed some short, but spectacular hikes to fuel the collective soul of the group so we packed up and headed a short drive up U.S. 219 and U.S. 50 north of Thomas to **Cathedral State Park** (304-735-3771, www.cathedralstatepark.com), home to a majestic 132-acre patch of old-growth eastern hemlock trees some as tall as 90 feet, as big around as 21 feet, and as old as 500 years.

It had been some time since we had hiked among this planet's elders. Jake and I got to hike among the ancient Sitka Spruce out in

Ecola Beach, Oregon, where they filmed "Goonies" a few years back, and that intense feeling of awe is one you don't forget.

On this hike, you could tell it was felt by everyone in our group from the baby to us juice-box-carrying Sherpas. Our necks craned to the heavens staring at these green giants that once covered the Appalachian Mountains. It was easy here, and knowing the state's modern day hell-bend for mountain destruction, that you were thankful that at least some people measure a man's worth by the number of things he can leave alone. Branson Haas, a hotel worker bought this land in 1922, and gave it to the state in 1942 on the stipulation that they never touch it with ax or saw.

Interestingly with the recent and dramatic March blasts of rain, it wasn't just the standing ancient trees that piqued our interest but Cathedral's moss-mountain laurel-fern-and-fungi-covered underbelly that was teeming with life often born out of the fallen giants on the forest floor.

After some swinging and sliding on the Cathedral playground, we figured we'd better roll back to Thomas for lunch before the kids gnawed down some timber.

Although with that many kids on board you normally wouldn't stop for nothing, it simply is impossible for any tourist to ramble past a sign that says, "Smallest Church in 48 States," without stopping. And thus, our caravan pulled over and said a few mini Hail Marys at **Our Lady of the Pines** (304-678-8171), the 24-foot-by-12-foot Catholic church that was built by Mr and Mrs. Peter Milkint of Eglon, W.Va., in 1957-1958, and that in 1972 (perhaps at the height of mini-church worship) saw 37,000 visitors from 48 states and 17 countries walk through its tiny doors.

After doing a little Bible reading in the front of the church (rightfully opened to Psalms 121, "I will lift up mine eyes to the hills"), we scrambled back down to the town of Thomas where we hit a quick lunch at **Flying Pigs** (134 East St. Thomas, 304-463-4292) a place known for its all-day breakfast, and recently named in the state's 101 Unique Places to Dine publication.

With bellies full we decided on one more short afternoon hike and what better place in the Valley to "shock and awe" some probably nap-time-ready little tikes than at the always-impressive **Blackwater Falls State Park** (304-259-5216, www.blackwaterfallsp.com).

With temps into the mid 70s, it seemed weird having been skiing all weekend, to be a day later at the Falls in March sans snow and where they only had their sledding run (according to the folks at the front desk in the gift shop) open only a couple times this season.

Lined with 20 miles of trails on both sides of the Blackwater Canyon, the park is a beautiful stop and the falls, one of those must-see places that all West Virginians should go see in any season.

We opted for the "stairmaster" edition hike, the boardwalks down to what I call "rootbeer falls," the five-story tall waterfall of frothing black water the result of tannic acid from fallen hemlock and red spruce needles.

There are pitfalls for sure to going to these places in between seasons, and in the Valley such iconic places as Purple Fiddle, Blackwater Brewing Company, etc., were all on winter hours, but we hiked that falls hike which is jam packed in summer with tourists, with only a handful of people including folks who'd eaten near us at Flying Pigs.

Approaching them with a now a sweaty beard full of cookie

crumbs, I assured them it was just coincidence, that we were not stalking them, and that we were not the walking dead, which, somehow made them walk faster.

Completely surrounded in the valley by the rugged beauty of Dolly Sods and the vast pockets of the sprawling **Monongahela National Forest** (http://www.fs.usda.gov/main/mnf/home), it was hard not to suggest just one more hike but our creekside cabin

complete with hot tub and a refrigerator stocked with some mountain made homebrew was calling. Besides, with only one day left in the valley, we were saving the best hike for last.

And by the best, this Griswold-idolizing family guy means, of course, the toughest, most grueling hike to test his family's sanity and friend's mettle.

So for our last ramble in the area, we convoyed about 25 miles over to the intersection of state routes 33 and 55, to **Seneca Rocks** (304-567-2827). While the Discovery Center won't open until April (weekends only until Memorial Day), we tracked down the nearest person in a funny hat who promptly pointed us in the vague direction of the bizarre white/gray Tuscarora quartzite formations that rise some 990 feet above the North Fork River.

In a rush to visit one of West Virginia's most famous sites we ambled off at a near Jacob Burcham pace, shutting not only the sunscreen but perhaps our brains back in the minivans as we'd filled our backpacks haphazardly with enough crackers to stock a courthouse vending machine and, with practically everything else but enough water. Tranced out by the increasingly closer 250-foot

thick slabs on these exposed ridges we (two college professors, three journalists and a tweener who'd read the three "Hunger Games" books in a weekend), somehow could not read these two words — "observation deck" with an arrow pointing the other direction.

So while we spent about an hour and a half exploring the creek, scrambling up steep and fun rockclimber trails and moseying up what became a closed road, we learned that we had not yet begun to hike.

Although we faced the reality of a 1,000-foot-climb, 1.5-mile climb with varying degrees of gratitude, (our oldest child winning the Oscar for best whining tweener in a dramatic series), I think everyone agreed later that we were all glad we'd stepped up to what seemed like the top of our West Virginia world.

Back down in the valley below, everyone now — after hiking hours without water — swears that those little two general stores are purveyors of what could possibly be best ice tea on the planet and that a Spring Break with both kinds of ramps - snowboard and the edible wild plant - is some kind of wonderful.

Let's Go Trippin: Canaan Valley

WHAT: The highest valley east of The Mississippi Canaan Valley is home to Timberline Four Seasons Resort, Canaan Valley Ski Resort, and White Grass, which has cross country and telemark skiing.

WHERE: Located about 3 1/2 hours north east of Huntington and about an hour north of Elkins.

WHERE TO STAY: Timberline Resort has ski-in, ski-out, Timberline Hotel, as well as ski-in, ski-out cabins slopeside, and hundreds of other cabin, condo and bunkhouse options at www.t4sr.com. Canaan Resort's Lodge underwent a $34 million renovation in fall 2013 with 160 new guest rooms and suites. Call 304-866-4121 or go online at www.canaanresort.com.

FOR MORE INFO: Go online at www.canaanvalley.org for more info.

Other Funky Festivals

Here's a look a just a few other unique festivals and events in the region:

Fasnacht in Helvetia: Helvetia, W.Va., was settled in 1869 by Swiss and German immigrants. Their descendants host the famous annual Fasnacht (think small town Mardi Gras) pre-lenten fest which has its roots in the Swiss Winterfest. Enjoy a parade of masks, dancing, music, traditional foods and a bonfire to burn an effigy of Old Man Winter. Visit www.helvetiawv.com for more info.

Mothman Festival: Point Pleasant, W.Va. hosts its annual Mothman Festival, celebrating the sightings of the winged Mothman creature in the late 1960s near the TNT site and just before the Silver Bridge collapse. Held the third Saturday in September the fest features paranormal, UFO, Bigfoot and other phenomena experts from around the world, as well, films, tours, and more. Go online at www.mothmanfestival.com for more info.

West Virginia Hot Dog Festival: Taking place at Pullman Square in Huntington, The WV Hot Dog Festival features wiener dog races, hot dog eating and root beer chugging contests, and a wealth of Tri-State hot dog vendors such as Stewart's, Hillbilly Hot Dogs, Midway, Frostop and more. The Fest takes place the last Saturday in July and raises money for the Hoops Family Children's Hospital at Cabell Huntington Hospital.

Washboard Festival: The Columbus Washboard Company in Logan, Ohio, gives the love to the Washboard every June at the Washboard Music Festival. Enjoy one of Ohio's most unique music tests as each band (from country and Cajun to world beat, blues and rock) utilizes the washboard in its band. Enjoy free tours of America's last washboard company. Go online at www.washboardmusicfestival.com for more info.

Ohio Paw Paw Festival: Held in Albany, Ohio at Lake Snowden, the 17th annual Paw Paw Festival will be in 2015. It celebrates one of America's largest native tree fruits, the Pawpaw (Asimina triloba). The event highlights the history and possibilities of the pawpaw. Enjoy competitions for best pawpaw-related work of art, pawpaw cook-off, and the ever-popular pawpaw-eating contest. There's also music, vendors, and presentations on topics related to sustainability. Visit www.ohiopawpawfest.com for more info.

WV Roadkill Cook-off: Located in Marlinton, W.Va., in late September, the Roadkill Cookoff is a world famous wild game cook-off that includes dishes with everything from squirrel and rabbit to bear and deer. In 2015, it will be the 23rd annual event. Go online at http://pccocwv.com/roadkill for more info.

Hillbilly Days: Held for more than 38 years in early to mid April in downtown Pikeville, Ky., Hillbilly Days draws in Shriners from all over North America to dress up, drive their jalopies in the unique parade and raise money for the Shriners Hospital in Lexington. Enjoy live bluegrass from such regional acts as Coaltown Dixie, arts and crafts, corn hole tournaments and more. Go online at http://www.hillbillydays.com

Blenko Glass Festival: Held each year in early August, the Blenko Glass Factory in Milton, opens up for a weekend of hands-on workshops letting folks make a wide array of glass ornaments, stained glass and other items. Watch demonstrations, speakers, do tours and get special signed, limited edition pieces from one of West Virginia's last hand-blown glass factories. Go online at www.blenkoglass.com for more info.

The 34th annual Irish Spring Festival: As featured on CBS Sunday Morning, The Irish Spring Festival, held around St. Patrick's Day weekend in March in Ireland, W.Va., is known for its Irish themed events including a greenery stroll, a snake chase, a blarney rock, a harping workshop and most famous of all, Irish Road Bowling. The first event of the more than 20 event season of the West Virginia Irish Road Bowlers Association, the Ireland event can draw hundreds of bowlers competing in the ancient Irish sport. Go online at http://www.angelfire.com/wv/irishspringfestival/ for more info on the festival.

West Virginia

BRAMWELL

Writing the weekly fall foliage report since late September, I have to confess that by last week I was getting a little leaf envy.

Each week, I've been writing about vibrant, color quilts of red, orange and yellow over in yonder mountains of West Virginia, while here in the low-lying Ohio River valley, the hills still look like a stadium full of green-shirted Marshall fans.

Not that there's anything wrong with that, but my leaf-peeping patience was waning.

And there's a road-trip for that.

We loaded the kids into our little red Saturn wagon (the one that Jake etched "no climb-ing" onto the car hood with a stone) and did just that, went car mountain climbing up, down and over to the wonderful little town of Bramwell, W.Va.

Located on the Bluestone River, and tucked into the mountains just north of Bluefield, W.Va. (and a stone's throw from the Virginia border), Bramwell is one little oddly-refreshing town.

Incorporated in 1888, Bramwell, located on U.S. 52, was once considered the richest, little town in the United States.

Between the town's birth and the Depression, which crushed the coal boom and closed the town's only bank, Bramwell had as many as 19 millionaires and boy did those coal barons build some houses.

Today, Bramwell with 18 super-sized mostly Victorian-style structures on its historic walking tour, vibes like Mayberry meets MTV's "Cribs" since even the carriage houses are as large as the houses most of us 'round here grew up in.

Not wanting to drive three hours just for a needed shot of fall foliage and a house tour, the Dave Trippin crew decided to hit

Bramwell last weekend for its 13th annual **Bramwell Oktoberfest** (www.bramwelloktoberfest.com) when the town's little brick streets and these giant, wrap-around porches were filled with the sounds of people, the flow of good brew and music from of some of the Mountain State's best artists including The Carpenter Ants, Todd Burge, John Lilly and a bevy of eclectic string bands.

Although we're normally tent campers and sometimes not even blow-up mattress tent campers, we figured that when in Rome we best get a lil' taste of how the other half lived.

In with another Huntington couple armed with rug-rats, we put up our eight-member crew for the weekend at **Victorian Elegance,** a B&B on Main Street that was built in 1911 and then refurbished by Larry and Molly Robinette, who also run **The River's Edge Bed and Breakfast** at the corner of South River and Brick Street (304-248-8543).

Molly, the former mayor who helped ignite the town's revival by even helping lure a bank back to Bramwell and by turning the River's Edge B&B and garden into something straight off of HGTV, has also done quite the job restoring Victorian Elegance, the old M. Abrahamson's store that once sold clothing, dry goods and "notions" -- whatever that is.

I had the notion that since the room we were staying in was the Princess Grace, that her descendants might saunter up and bring us breakfast in bed for the price we'd paid.

While that dream was deferred, we did get an amazing, heaped-on breakfast from **Bramwell Cafe** 304-248-7414 that sent up enough eggs, bacon, biscuits and sausage to make Bob Evans blush at the bounty.

On the second morning we were treated to breakfast at River's Edge with Molly, Larry and their almost Dr. Doolittle-like home filled with lovable Great Danes, parrots, cats and pictures of even wilder animals.

Throughout our three-day weekend in Bramwell, I couldn't help but just keep walking around and gawking.

Rachel Booth, who was working at the restored train depot for the Coal Heritage Highway Authority, said everything was within walking distance, and she wasn't kidding.

The Oktoberfest, which sold more than 1,000 tickets pre-sale for its one-day event, ran for only a few blocks down Bramwell's brick streets. Bramwell's staggering wealth of homes is all packed in a tight circle that's boiling over with history.

A hot spot for that history is the replica train depot that was built in the late 1990s.

While 14 trains a day once stopped in this town when coal was king, the **Bramwell Depot** (866-858-8959) is now a museum, gift shop and hub for visitors who have (thanks to fellow ink-stained wretches) been trickling in this summer from all over Virginia, West Virginia, Kentucky, New York, Ohio, Florida and even Wisconsin.

Booth said events such as Oktoberfest, which featured a tour bus of folks from Charleston, is essential to turning tourists onto the goodness in their own backyard, and along the Coal Heritage Highway, a National Scenic Byway, that goes along U.S. 52 to Welch and then along West Virginia 16 in Ansted.

"One of the most intact coal communities is right here," Booth said. "I was talking to a lady who came here just the other day because she grew up in a coal town but it is not there anymore.

People move away and leave homes, and then a lot of those towns no longer exist."

In Bramwell you get the sense that the little town is being rediscovered and getting some "This Old House" kind of love and attention put back into the houses.

Rory Perry, who also lives in Charleston, has been one of the guys who moved into town and has helped out with the Oktoberfest that is hosted by George and Lara Sitler.

Started as small as it gets, the Oktoberfest drew in an amazing array of micobreweries from Georgia, North Carolina, Virginia, Kentucky, Ohio, West Virginia and Brewery Ommegang, from Cooperstown, N.Y. In all, they showcased some 69 different brews.

"It's been a pleasure to be a part of this and to watch it grow and to see the town embrace the Oktoberfest," said Perry, right after The Carpenter Ants fired up "Georgia On A Fast Train" with a little gal playing washboard for them. "It started as a way to support West Virginia microbreweries, and it's grown beyond West Virginia's borders and now is almost a family reunion."

The Lavender crew certainly found that to be true.

Former Huntington residents, Berdawn Hutchinson and James Bach, drove down from Columbus to enter Czarina's Imperial Stout (James' first homebrew) into the competition and to get a taste of West Virginia on the weekend of the couple's 12th wedding anniversary.

One of Ommegang's brewers, Wes Nick, a Wheeling native

who has been with the Cooperstown, N.Y., Belgium brewery for 2 1/2 years, drove the farthest to take part in Oktoberfest at Bramwell.

"It's a long haul," Nick said, at the Oktoberfest awards ceremony. "I was about 11 hours into it and I was starting to get skeptical and thinking, 'What's really going to be going on here?' But this is phenomenal. I was blown away. I mean, here I am back in my home state, representing."

Although the Lavender contingent on Saturday had found the Bramwell Caboose geocache, walked lots and danced plenty in the brick streets to such bands as The Carpenter Ants and Huntington's own, Big Rock and the Candyass Mountain Boys, we gave a Sunday morning send-off to Bramwell and lit off under more blue skies for a nice day-hike at nearby **Pinnacle Rock State Park** (304-248-8565).

Located directly up the mountain on U.S. 52 from Bramwell, Pinnacle Rock looks like a giant, sandstone Lego construction that almost unnaturally juts some 3,100 feet above sea level.

Opened in 1938, this most unusual day park, boasts an impressive picnic shelter with stone fireplace that was constructed by the Works Progress Administration (WPA) in conjunction with the state of West Virginia.

Once only 26 acres, the park has grown to nearly 400 acres and is a great day hike (with several geocaches located nearby). We figured we'd best explore.

From the Homestead and Acorn Ridge Trails you get a better view from the bottom of that bizarre sandstone ridge and how it lays jagged on top the mountain.

Oddly enough our hike to Jimmy Lewis Lake found the lake totally sucked dry of water, leaving nothing but a lake bed of mud. Mud, which claimed one of Jake's shoes and tried to suck in my hiking shoes, overall pants and a nice portion of my pride.

A whole lot muddy, a bit tired, a bit hungry and a whole lot barefoot, we started our three-hour drive back to Huntington through the fiery foliage of Southern West Virginia gazing at God's quilt of many colors.

Finally starting to laugh about our muddy adventures, we were glad to get a sneak peek at that fall color and to make it to the amazing, little town of Bramwell, where everything -- even the bottom of the lake -- is within walking distance.

Let's Go Trippin: Bramwell

OKTOBERFEST: 2015 will be the 20th anniversary of Bramwell Oktoberfest, founded and ran by George and Lara Sitler and friends. Enjoy regional craft brews and an eclectic mix of live bands playing on porches, and on the streets. Go online at www.bramwelloktoberfest.com

OTHER EVENTS: Bramwell hosts historic home tours a couple times a year including a Christmas Tour of Homes. and A Twilight Ghost Walk in Historic Bramwell.

GOOD STUFF NEARBY: Pinnacle Rock State Park, Holiday of Lights Display in Bluefield, the Princeton Railroad Museum, the Pocahontas Exhibition Mine (Pocahontas, Va.), Winterplace Ski Resort.

WHERE TO STAY: The historic town is filled with Bed and Breakfast options. Call 304-248-7414 or go online at http://Bramwellrentals.com/ for more info.

MORE INFO: Stop by the Coal Heritage Interpretative Center, located off U.S. 52 in Bramwell at the old train depot. Call 304-248-8595. Go online at http://www.bramwellwv.com for more info. Also, visit the Mercer County Convention and Visitors Bureau online at http://www.visitmercercounty.com/

ALONG THE WAY: The scenic route to Bramwell is by taking U.S. 52 south to Bramwell. That's going to take a while. The quicker route is I-64 to Charleston and then I-77 to 460 west at Princeton to County Road 123 west to U.S. 52.

If you travel I-77, be sure to stop by "Tamarack: The Best of West Virginia," where you can enjoy fresh-made and reasonably-priced food made by the chefs of the Greenbrier. Go online at www.tamarackwv.com.

Other Beer Fests

Here's a look at some other cool craft beer festivals in the region.

Rails And Ales: Celebrating its third year in 2015 on August 15, the Rails and Ales Festival will be held at Harris Riverfront Park and is organized by the Better Beer Coalition. The fest sold out the first two years and features live music, food from local restaurants, artisan vendors, and specialty craft beer from West Virginia breweries and craft breweries across the US and from around the world. The fest is part of the new West Virginia Craft Beer Week,

and Huntington Craft Beer Week, a full week of beer launch events, beer pairing dinners, pub bicycle rides and more. Go online at www.railsandales.com and www.wvcbw.com for more info.

Rails, Trails and Ales: Runs in early August for a weekend in the Ohio River city of Marietta, Ohio, home to the Marietta Brewing Company. Enjoy a weekend of craft brews spiced with paddles (including a dice run and an anything that floats race) on the nearby Muskingum River, as well as road, trail and family bicycle rides all weekend long. Go online at www.rtafest.com for more info.

Brew Skies: Organized by Mountain State Brewing Company in Davis, Brew Skies is held in late August (Aug. 22 2015) at

Timberline Four Seasons Resort in Canaan Valley and features lots of regional craft breweries, as well as local foods, and two dozen eclectic regional and nationally-traveling music acts, hikes and more. Go online at www.brewskiesfestival.com for more info.

Oktoberfest Zinzinnati: Held for three days in late September in downtown Cincinnati, Zinzinnati is hailed as the largest Oktoberfest celebration in the country. More than half-a-million herren und frauen will converge on a six-block area of Fifth Street to eat, sing, mingle, sport lederhosen, listen to polka music, try to speak German and perform the Chicken Dance. Go online at http://www.oktoberfestzinzinnati.com/

River Valley Craft Beer Fest: Had its first fest in September 2014 in Portsmouth, Ohio on the lot at The Party Connection which houses over 500 craft beers, 1800 wines, and 200 premium cigars. Had a dozen breweries, local food and music. Go online at http://www.thepartyconnectiononline.net/ for more info.

Ohio Brew Week: Held in Athens, Ohio, Ohio Brew Week celebrates its 10th year in July 2015. While the main focus is craft brew, there is also events featuring local wineries, meaderies, distilleries, and cideries. Enjoy a full week of events, dinners, speakers, live music, local food and more. Go online at www.ohiobrewweek.com.

Ashland Fest of Ales: Ashland in Motion is hosting an inaugural Fest of Ales on June 20, 2015 in downtown Ashland, Ky. Go online at www.ashlandinmotion.org for more info.

Great River Craft Brew Festival: Held on April 25, 2015 at the historic Ro-Na Theatre in downtown Ironton. This was a first year beer fest that featured a number of Buckeye State microbreweries such as Portsmouth Brewing Company, Jackie O's, out of Athens; The Brew Kettle out of Strongsville, Ohio, Great Lakes Brewing out of Cleveland and along with breweries from surrounding states. Go online at https://www.facebook.com/GreatRiverBeerFest?ref=br_tf for more info.

West Virginia

HATFIELDS & MCCOYS

Millions tuned in a couple years ago to watch the History Channel miniseries "Hatfields & McCoys" about the famous feuding families from West Virginia and Kentucky.

The six-hour miniseries aired after the debut of the companion two-hour documentary "America's Greatest Feud: Hatfields and McCoys" that aims to share the real story with lots of local experts and reenactors.

Heritage Farm Museum and Village was used as the filming set for a dozen scenes featured in the documentary. Huntington-based Trifecta Productions did the filming and several locals served as re-enactors. In addition, the documentary utilizes such historians as former Gov. Paul Patton, Nancy Cade and Reed Potter from Kentucky and Fred Armstrong, Raamie Barker, Bill Richardson and Keith Davis from West Virginia to tell the story as clips of re-enactors play out scenes that stoked America's most famous family feud.

The documentary is directed by the late Mark Cowen, who is known for the documentary "Band of Brothers: We Stand Alone Together" and "Magnificent Desolation: Walking on the Moon 3-D," among other things.

Milton native and Marshall University graduate Darrell Fetty, who produced both the documentary and miniseries, said he was elated at the level of work in both films.

Cowen said by phone from California that everyone at the production company ThinkFactory was ecstatic at the success of the miniseries whose Memorial Day premiere pulled in a new record 13.9 viewers for a cable network debut (non-sports), and excited to share the documentary.

"They did a great job, and so now it is my job to try and fill in the spots where there may still be questions and maybe fill it out more for people who watched the miniseries," Cowen said. "That said, whoever watched the miniseries knows 50 times more than the last person who looked into the 'Hatfields and McCoys' because I think the common man who read anything about this in grade school thought it was a fight about a pig."

To flesh out the clearest and truest story about the feud, Cowen said they pinball back and forth between Kentucky and West Virginia's bevy of historians as well as utilizing two books that take a deep look into the undertow of the feud that was soaked in the blood of the Civil War and socioeconomic issues of the day. The books were Altina L. Waller's "Feud: Hatfields, McCoys, and Social Change in Appalachia, 1860-1900," as well as "The Feud: The All-American, No-Holds-Barred, Blood-and-Guts Story of The Hatfields and McCoys," a new book by Richmond, Va.-based writer Dean King.

Weaving in old photos, maps and the re-enactment footage, Cowen said he and Paul Peltekian, who helped edit and produce, try to tell a balanced tale utilizing in-depth interviews.

"I was given the task from a documentary standpoint of trying to come up with the story that at least gives balance to both the Hatfields and the McCoys by talking to the scholars with different opinions," Cowen said. "Darrell set out with this to say there is two stories to this and if we don't tell two stories we've failed. So we tried to reach out to as many scholars and descendants and authors as we could."

With no footage of the actual participants and few photographs, Cowen breathed new life into the feud by utilizing Trifecta Productions to shoot two-days of re-enactments at Heritage Farm.

With a tiny budget that called for a re-enactment with one horse, a handful of guns and four or five actors, Trifecta Vice President Joe Murphy got on the phone and rallied scores of re-enactors and niche experts -- horsemen such as Huntington Mayor Kim Wolfe and Barboursville Police Chief Mike Coffey, veteran Civil War re-enactors and weapons experts such as Thadd McClung, Clarence Craigo, Ron McClintock, Bill Hunt and Bob Walden, wardrobes from the Marshall University Theater Department, Western Virginia Military Academy and Civil War and

pioneer era seamstresses such as Jo Patterson, who made dresses solely for the shoot.

Cowen said he was blown away by Trifecta's ability to gather Hollywood-level resources quickly and economically.

"As a director you ask for something and hope that gets done but this, this is just classic Joe Murphy," Cowen said. "He has the No. 1 thing you asked for then has two or three just in case you

need it. That was at every turn. I needed five extras he said 'here's 10 that you can pick from.' I asked for one horse we get eight. That was unexpected."

Trifecta President Jack Reynolds said the company is proud to be part of a project.

"Riding on the coat tails of the tremendous success of the 'Hatfields & McCoys' miniseries, the documentary has the ability to shed an in-depth accuracy to the myth and legend of this world famous feud," said Reynolds. "Validated by its mere alliance with The History Channel, this historical reference is enlightening and guides the viewer to the complexity of the entire story. I personally have learned many new facts and clarified other details that have been told incorrectly throughout the past. The fact that this entire event happened in our own back yard was in itself compelling for me to watch and participate in all of the hype, but the fact that this documentary, in its near entirety, was filmed locally by Huntington's own Trifecta Productions with local actors and re-enactors, has the entire community committed to it's success. This is just another example of the natural resources that West Virginia and the Tri-State community has to offer and the tremendous talent that is here for the taking."

The region's Civil War re-enactment community also came out to help. State award-winning history teacher Michael Sheets of Huntington Middle School brought some of his older Western Virginia Military Academy students (a Civil War re-enacting unit) along with extra clothes and a trunk of brogans for use.

Cabin Creek, W.Va., resident Jimmy Rogers, a coal miner and Civil War re-enactor since 2001, was picked to play Paris McCoy.

"I just came out for the chance to do it," Rogers said. "Everybody wants that little taste of being in a movie and something like this."

Rogers said since he works midnights at a subsidiary of Patriot Coal, he was able to take the time off.

"It's been a great experience," Rogers said. "At re-enactments you normally don't get this much attention to detail. It is just like you see in the movies. This might not have the budget of a Hollywood blockbuster but you see that they work just as hard to make sure every expression and every composure is right."

Red Dog Monroe, a regular re-enactor at such events as the Way Back Weekends at Heritage Farm and at the upcoming Old Central City Days, said the documentary is a refreshing change for West Virginia's stories in film.

"It's nice to see a West Virginia story about West Virginians told by West Virginians with a crew in West Virginia," Monroe said. "It makes you feel good to be involved in something like this. They contacted us and we just started pulling everybody out."

While Cowen said there is no way to know the exact truth of what happened, he hopes that folks who watch the documentary get a fuller understanding of a tragic American story.

Cowen, a lifelong student of history, is excited that people are responding to a real story and going further into the heart of it.

"Every once in a while you go back into history and find the right story and people are ready for it," Cowen said. "I think honestly the miniseries as well as the documentary makes you want to pick up a book and read more about it. I'm a bibliophile, so I would love to be able to play a small part in all of that."

Let's Go Trippin: Hatfields and McCoys

WHAT: Heritage Farm's Way Back Weekend has a Hatfield and McCoy-themed event every summer featuring the reenactors from the History Channel documentary. The 2015 event will be in August.

WHERE: Heritage Farm Museum and Village, located at 3300 Harvey Road, Huntington.

WHAT ELSE: The national award-winning Heritage Farm features more than 15 restored log cabin buildings including a blacksmith shop, a church, a country store, a barn (with petting zoo). There's daily tours of the Museum of Progress, Museum of Transportation and the Country Store Museum are available to the

public all year, Monday through Saturday from 10 a.m. to 3 p.m. The last tour begins at 2 p.m. (Except for major holidays and in the months of December, January and February, tours are available, weather permitting). New attractions include the new doll museum, a new cafe and welcome center, a group overnight retreat facility, and caboose B&Bat the farm which was announced in 2015 as the first Smithsonian affiliate in West Virginia.

CONTACT: Call 304-523-6115 or go online at http://www.heritagefarmmuseum.com/

More Feudin'

Here's some other ways and places to dig into Hatfields and McCoys history.

Hatfield-McCoy Reunion Festival: The second weekend of June in downtown Williamson, W.Va. The fest attracts people come from all over the US. The festival features lots of family friendly things to do including: music, plays, tours of the Hatfield McCoy Feud sites, a tug-of-war across the Tug river by descendants of the feuding families, golf tournament, ATV poker run, great home cooking and lots of other fun – all with a Hatfield McCoy Feud theme. It also coincides with the Hatfield-McCoy Marathon and is centered near several trailheads for the Hatfield-McCoy ATV trails. Call 304)-235-5240

Hatfield and McCoy Feud Tours: In Pikeville, Ky., you can take a self-guided audio driving tour. There is also a guided bus tour and a feud app that directs you to feud sties using your Smart phone. Go online at http://www.tourpikecounty.com/ hatfields_and_mccoys/ to find out more about the tours or contact Pike County Tourism CVB at (800) 844-7453. Tour schedule is subject to change. Tours leave out from the Pike County Tourism Office in the Hampton Inn off of 831 Hambley Blvd., Pikeville

Hatfield/McCoy Airboat Tours: Based out of the Matewan Depot, near the bridge in downtown Matewan, they offer rides on the Tug River. Tours also can be arranged by appointment on Sunday afternoons and Mondays. Groups of three or more are encouraged. The boat carries a maximum of six passengers per tour. See wildlife and enjoy the scenery while your guide fills you in on local history about feuding, moonshining, coal mining and more. Call 304-928-7702. Also feel free to connect on their Facebook page

West Virginia

SNOWTUBING

Achia Brockington has worn a path between hospitals and home as her 6-year-old daughter Shydae Brown battles Hodgkin's Lymphoma.

But Martin Luther King, Jr., Weekend, the little lady with a bright pink snow suit and million dollar smile got to go down a carefree country road less traveled — the wild, wonderful snowtubing lanes of snowy West Virginia.

Along with Brockington's fiancé, Alex Johnson, and other friends in the Special Love group from D.C., the Baltimore family were some of the many people who got to try out the brand new snowtubing park at Canaan Valley Resort State Park.

"It has been a trial and a devastating experience dealing with her illness so seeing her so full of life has been great,"

Brockington said. "We left all the stress and are trying to just enjoy life. We don't have to worry about it and all the back and forth to the hospitals. This clears your mind."

Although not all dressed as stylish as Shydae, kids of all ages, even ones with gray hair, have been enjoying the two-hour tubing sessions at Canaan's Tube Park that opened Friday, Jan. 11, 2013.

On MLK Weekend hundreds of folks drove up the hill to the new tubing area that has a 1,200-feet-long run that now has five open lanes but which has space for up to 10 lanes.

Unlike tubing and sledding at home, there's no slogging your sled back up the hill through a foot-deep snow while warming up means gathering around the outside plaza fire ring or stepping inside the massive stone 1,000-square-foot warming station that features a fireplace, lounge areas, bathrooms and a concession stand.

With a panoramic view of Canaan Valley, tubers travel up a Boardwalk conveyor belt or Magic Carpet while scanning the view that included MLK Weekend being able to watch skiers carving powder Canaan, as well as a group of horseback riders from Timberline Stables making their way through the woods.

On his way back up to the top, New Hampshire native Josh Morrison, 32, who now lives in Elkins, said being out playing in the snow was something they had been craving this winter.

"It's definitely a blast, and it's extra handy for us," said Morrison, who was out with a group of 14 folks from the First United Methodist youth group. "We're from New Hampshire so we're used to the snow and being out in the winter. This year, we've not gotten much snow and we've talked to our family in New Hampshire and they're not having no snow at all either. Coming over for tubing is something that everyone can do and it's fun for everyone — even the 32-year-olds. We all like it."

That youth group — with kids as young as Morrison's 7-year-old daughter Katie and as old as, well all the adults in the group, is typical of tubing parks where folks of all ages unlock their inner child.

Elkins resident, Robert White said that while his wife, a school teacher, and kids have been tubing, he was always working and had never gotten to go — until just a few weekends ago.

You could say he was hooked on the feeling.

With the two-hour time slot waning, there was time for one last ride and White wasn't hanging out at the fire ring or inside the warming station.

Nope, he grabbed his tube rope and led the charge over to the conveyor-belt lift with his family and a slew of friends who decided to caravan over for a family fun day at the tubing park.

White was still laughing about his tube flipping over when he was doing a three-tube-train ride down with his daughter Ashley and wife, Jessica.

"I almost made it to the end — then my tube flipped over," White said laughing. "I never thought a 54-year-old man would have fun like this but we've all had a blast. I'm really glad we came here to do this. It's a nice thing for families to do together."

Creating that holistic experience for families is important for all West Virginia's downhill ski resorts, said Terry Pfeiffer, president of the West Virginia Ski Area Association.

No one would know better than Pfeiffer, who is president at Winterplace, which opened West Virginia's largest snow tubing park in 1997-1998 and continues to be a huge draw for the resort, located just minutes south of Beckley and just off of I-77.

Pfeiffer said it's like the best of backyard sledding since there's a warm lodge at the bottom of the hill complete with a fireplace, hot chocolate and food and two Magic Carpet lifts to take your tube back to the top.

"When we were all kids we went out sledding and you'd sled down those long hills and then guess what, you had to lug your sled back up," Pfeiffer said. "We have two Super Carpet lifts so you get to do it over and over again."

While skiing and snowboarding are still the main draws at Winterplace, Pfeiffer said having substantial tubing parks at Winterplace, Snowshoe (Silver Creek) and Canaan Valley helps everyone in on the winter fun.

"We all want to make it a great experience for everyone who comes to our resorts," Pfeiffer said. "As far as a family experience it's really great because everybody really can do it, great grandmas and great grandpas, grandmas and grandpas, moms and dads and kids. It really is something for everybody."

More Places To Go Snowtubing:

Here's a look at the places in the region where you can go snow tubing or sledding at public facilities.

Canaan Valley Resort State Park, Davis, W.Va.
In Davis, W.Va., about 180 miles northeast of Charleston, and just north of Elkins. It's about four to four-and-a-half hours from Huntington. The tubing park at Canaan Valley Resort is the longest tube park in the Mid-Atlantic region. Complete with rentals, warming hut, concessions and fireplace, the five-lane tubing park with the magic carpet mountaintop access.
Visit canaanresort.com or call 304-866-4121.

Silver Creek at Snowshoe Mountain, Snowshoe, W.Va.
Located in Snowshoe in Pocahontas County, about four to four-and-a-half hours from Huntington.
Silver Creek has 17 trails and the five-lane Coca Cola Tube Park. Call 877-441-4FUN or go online at www.snowshoemtn.com.

Winterplace, Flat Top, W.Va.
Winterplace, the closest ski resort to Huntington, is located two minutes south of Beckley off I-77, Exit 28, in Ghent/Flat Top, W.Va. About two-and-a-half hours from Huntington. With the user-friendly Super Carpet Lifts, it is an ideal place for little kids and beginners. Winterplace also a Snowtubing Park with two Super Carpet Lifts, and there are nine lifts. Call 800-607-SNOW or go online at www.winterplace.com

Blackwater Falls State Park
Located in Davis, W.Va., about 4 1/2 hours from Huntington, Blackwater Falls State Park has a new quarter-mile-long natural snow sled run that usually opens in December and runs through late winter. (mid March). It's known for its annual February Duct Tape and Cardboard Sled Race. There's also 10 miles of crosscountry trails nearby as well. Find out more about the Sled Run at www.BlackwaterFalls.com or call Blackwater Falls Nature Center at 304-259-4833, 9 a.m. to 4 p.m., or email blackwaterfallssp@wv.gov.

Ohio

'A CHRISTMAS STORY' HOUSE

Yes, Virginia, I am a 40-year-old shopping virgin.

After every Thanksgiving, my three sisters hunt and gather with the steam and elbows-out grace of a roller derby team -- chugging coffee, battling crowds and grabbing door buster specials before sunrise on Black Friday.

Sometimes those great deals and giant, flat-screen TVs even fit in their vans, and they don't have to call me at 4:47 a.m. begging for someone to bring a bigger van.

While I have never once given in to the temptation of getting Wal-Marted after Thanksgiving, I sure have my own holiday weaknesses.

When it comes to silly and fun holiday traditions you don't have to triple dog dare me to sit down and gift myself "a major award" -- getting to watch the 1983 Christmas classic, "A Christmas Story," a good four or five times with the family.

So loaded down with kids and coats, the Dave Trippin' mobile (with only a couple wrong turns) made a Thanksgiving-weekend trip back from my in-laws in upstate New York and into the quiet Tremont neighborhood near downtown Cleveland.

At 3159 W. 11th St., in Cleveland sits the honey mustard-colored, "A Christmas Story" house (www.AChristmasStoryHouse.com) where director/producer Bob Clark and crew filmed the iconic movie back in 1983 breathing life into Indiana native Jean Shepherd's quirky book about the adventures of Ralphie Parker called, "In God We Trust: All Others Pay Cash."

Pitched as an "original, traditional, 100-percent, red-blooded, two-fisted, All-American Christmas" story, the movie only took home a box office bank of $16 million (Harry Potter made that in about five minutes), but somehow the movie, which offered a promise of "Peace. Harmony. Comfort and Joy ... Maybe next year," cussed, snorted and shot its way into the hearts of the rest of America's dysfunctional families.

On the Saturday after Thanksgiving, we found the street teeming with "Ralphies" or fans who'd made a pilgrimage to Cleveland to see where many exterior scenes of the movie were filmed.

Bought on eBay for $150,000 and painstakingly restored by San Diego native Navy veteran, Brian Jones, the "A Christmas Story" house was opened to visitors on Thanksgiving weekend four years ago.

By Aug. 27, 2009, more than 100,000 people had been through the house.

For a nominal fee (now $10 and $6 for children 7 to 12) folks can (now open seven days a week) be armed with an info-rich self-guided tour pamphlet and be set loose in the house where immediately you run into the almost life-sized wooden box, marked "Fragile," which must be Italian, as old-man Parker said in the film.

Just a few steps into the famous movie house and just about everyone seems to happily roll back their age to that of pre-teens Ralphie and Randy Parker.

A college-age kid well over six-feet-tall opens a tiny kitchen cabinet door and twists, turns and folds himself under the sink and in his best

Randy voice cries to his mom's video camera, "Daddy's gonna kill Ralphie."

Everyone takes turns filing upstairs and packing into the boys' sailboat-covered red wallpapered bedroom where Ralphie wove nightly dreams of his Christmas lust for an "Official Red Ryder Carbine-Action Two-Hundred-Shot Range Model Air Rifle."

"Nice and toasty for a house this old," remarked an elderly lady who happened to be crammed in Ralphie's tiny room with about a dozen people peering at Ralphie's glasses sitting on the notebook where his epic letter to Santa still sat on a desk.

Of course, downstairs the highlight was getting to plop down on one of the two couches to drink in the glow of Cleveland-fried

Hollywood Christmas magic -- the present-laden Christmas tree from the set, where Randy and Ralphie "plunged into the cornucopia quivering with desire and the ecstasy of unbridled avarice" and, of course, framed perfectly in the main picture window, the Leg Lamp, which Ralphie called "the soft glow of electric sex gleaming in the window."

While the house is open all year-long, there is indeed something special about visiting this time of year.

While we were there on Thanksgiving weekend, the place was crawling with folks who'd been in the movie, as well as many folks who worked behind-the-scenes on either the movie, or in putting together the house and museum.

While seven of the original cast members, including Ian Petrella (Randy), Scott Schwartz (Flick), Tedde Moore (Miss Shields), Zack Ward (Scut Farkus), Yano Anaya (Grover Dill), Patty Johnson (Head Elf) and Drew Hocevar (Male Elf), were making appearances as part of the now annual Thanksgiving weekend convention, Petrella, will still be at the house starting Dec. 11, through sometime in January to give a behind-the-scenes perspective.

Across the street from the Parker family home, guests can tour the museum to see original movie props and costumes, including Randy's "I-can't-get-my-arms-down" snowsuit, and visit the gift shop to take home BB guns, bunny suits and their own major award (whether it be a leg lamp mug, T-shirt, pint-glasses, ornament or the real thing).

Inside the museum where a map is crammed with colorful stick pins representing visitors from some 42 countries, we ran into not only some sweet vintage props (such as Scut Farkus' sweet fur hat),

but also folks such as Jim Moralevitz, who "babysat" for the kid actors (ages 7 through 12) for the 29 days of filming in Cleveland and Toronto.

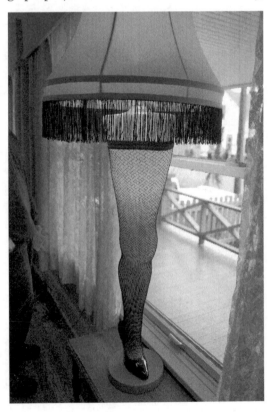

"Oh boy oh boy those kids were something else," Moralevitz told a packed crowd. "We did have a joyous time in those 29 days. Those boys were from California and had never saw snow, so it was like a gun for Peter (the snow blowers). He'd build the biggest mountains of snow

and wouldn't even let Randy try it."

With visions of little blond California kid Peter Billingsley shooting up this Cleveland neighborhood with a snow gun, and pelting director Bob Clark and his movie father, Darren McGavin with snowballs, we ran into another "Ralphie," or fan, who has ended up impacting the museum in a mighty way.

Canadian resident Tyler Schwartz, who was at the house talking to folks about he and his wife, Jordie's documentary film, "Road Trip for Ralphie," ended up spending two years sniffing around Ontario (where most of the movie was filmed) finding all its costumes in an old warehouse. And as if there need be any more evidence of Christmas miracles, was able to save the chalkboard and many other school props from the Victoria School in St. Catharines, Ontario, the day before the school was to be demolished.

Schwartz also told the Chippawa Volunteer Fire Department (Niagara Falls, Ontario), which owns and maintains the fire truck seen in the film, about their truck's storied history, and now the department crosses the border once a year or so to give folks rides through the neighborhood.

While Schwartz could have sold all of his finds to the museum, he ended up donating the items to the house and its museum, and has since received his own kind of Christmas-charged karma as they made Schwartz the sole Canadian dealer for leg lamps through his Retro Festival company of movie memorabilia.

Although it was tempting to drive just about five minutes from "A Christmas Story" where the Cleveland Indians baseball team has finally -- and not until the off-season -- found something productive to do with their diamond, a snow tubing, ice-skating adventure land called Snow Days, our hearts were long for the hills of home.

With a tired winter sun setting, we pulled onto I-77 south, where somewhere into the heart of that Mountain State darkness there glowed our own major award -- a family drive-through stop-off on the way home to the trains, reindeer, Mothman and jumping ATVs of the 7th annual Winterfest at Ripley's Cedar Lakes Conference Center (www.cedarlakes.com).

So with Cleveland in the rear-view mirror we took turns passing around the nasty-tasting LifeBuoy bar of soap, laughed at our leg lamp ornament, then sliced open our "Oh Fudge," passing around the bounty and giving thanks for crazy dreamers like Brian Jones, and for collective Christmas wishing.

To twist a line from "A Christmas Story's" trailer, there may not be peace, harmony, comfort and joy but who knows, maybe next year.

Let's Go Trippin: A Christmas Story

WHAT: "A Christmas Story" house is the house where one of the most popular Christmas movies, "A Christmas Story," was filmed in 1983. In addition to the house, visitors can explore the gift shop and a separate museum where items from the movie and more than 100 behind-the-scenes photos are displayed.

WHERE: 3159 W. 11th St., Cleveland, Ohio (just minutes from downtown Cleveland) in the quaint Tremont neighborhood. Drive time is about five hours from Huntington.

HOW MUCH: $10, children 7 to 12 are $6 and kids 6 and under get in free.

WHEN: Open year-round. They are closed Easter, Thanksgiving, Christmas, New Year's Day and all other major holidays. Hours are extended during the Christmas season.

GET INFO: www.achristmasstoryhouse.com and call 216-298-4919.

WHAT ELSE: They sponsor a Christmas Story 5 and 10K run in early December. In its fourth year in 2015. Asian-American Bistro and Bar is the official Chinese restaurant of "A Christmas Story House." It is located a few blocks away at 2661 W. 14th Street, Cleveland, Ohio.

LIGHTS ALONG THE WAY: There are some great lights off of I-77, including the 800,000 lights that make up the annual Winterfest Lighting Display at Cedar Lakes Conference Center, just off the Ripley/Fairplain exit 132). That display includes a covered bridge in lights. Go online at www.cedarlakes.com or call 304-372-7873.

DAVE'S TOP 5 AREA LIGHT PICKS: Wheeling's Oglebay lights, St. Albans Festival of Lights, a double-shot of Ashland's Winter Wonderland of Lights, and Paul Porter Park's lights in Coal Grove, Ohio, and Winterfest at Cedar Lakes in Ripley, W.Va.

Other Cool TV/Movie Sites:

Here's a few cool movie and TV location sites to check out.

We Are Marshall: The Warner Brothers film was shot all over Huntington. Some prime sports are the Memorial Fountain at the Marshall Memorial Student Center, Spring Hill Cemetery, the Keith-Albee, the Frederick Hotel as well as the Bus Depot. Go online at www.herald-dispatch.com to click onto the Marshall plane crash web site to find out more.

Mothman: The 2001 film, "The Mothman Prophecies," was shot in Pa., but you can go to where Mothman was seen, and find out everything about the film and see props and memorabilia from the film, by visiting The Mothman Museum, 411 Main St., Point Pleasant. The Museum also runs regular bus tours to the TNT area. Jeff Wamsley and the Museum also helps put on the annual Mothman Festival. It will celebrate its 14th year in 2015. Go online at www.mothmanmuseum.com for more info.

Huntington's Kitchen: 911 Third Ave., Huntington, originally established as "Jamie's Kitchen," during the TV production of the first season of "Jamie Oliver's Food Revolution." Oliver wanted to see the kitchen remain open to the public which it still is. Stop by the unique kitchen now run by Cabell Huntington Hospital and which houses a wide array of cooking classes, demos, and events. Call 304-522-0887 or go online at http://www.huntingtons-kitchen.org/

Loretta Lynn's Homeplace: Located about 60 miles from Huntington (south on U.S. 23) in Van Lear, Ky., is Butcher Hollow where Country Music legend Loretta Lynn was born and raised. Lynn's life was captured in the 1980 biopic, "Coal Miner's Daughter," for which Sissy Spacek won an Oscar. Tour the home featured in the film and stop by the Webb's Grocery nearby that is owned by Loretta's brother Herman.

Super 8: Weirton, West Virginia, was the small-town setting for the 2011 film "Super 8." A perfect fit for this sci-fi film set in the 1970's, the town welcomed director J.J. Abrams and made Hollywood feel at home. Check out area restaurants such as Cathy's Pies and Sandwiches, DeStefano's as well as the neighborhood Avenue F. Go online at http://www.wvcommerce.org/travel/journal/super8onlocation.aspx for more info about visiting the sites.

Matewan/Tad Hamilton: See two of the WV's movie landmarks in one day with a rafting trip on the New River. John Sayles' 1986 film, "Matewan,"was shot in Thurmond, W.Va. And at the take-out for the Lower New, pass under the world-famous New River Gorge Bridge that was in the 2003 Dreamworks film, "Win a Date with Tad Hamilton."

Shawshank Redemption: Built in 1886, the Ohio State Reformatory, at Mansfield, Ohio (just above Columbus) served for a prison for 94 years. It perhaps is most famous as it was used as a movie set for prisons in "Air Force One," "Tango and Cash," and most famously, "Shawshank Redemption," which was shot in 1994, and which just celebrated a 20-year anniversary party in 2014.

Hillbilly Hot Dogs: Located at 6951 Ohio River Road, Lesage, has been featured on such TV shows as Guy Fieri's "Diners, Drive-Ins, and Dives," the Food Network's "The Road," the Travel Channel's "101 Tastiest Places to Chow Down," and several other shows. Call 304-762-2458 or 304-522-0044 for more info or go online at www.hillbillyhotdogs.com

Ohio

CINCINNATI ZOO

On the Saturday of Memorial Day weekend, daredevil Robbie "Kaptain" Knievel jumped over 24 delivery trucks (more than 200 feet) at Kings Island.

Not bad Kaptain -- for flying solo.

That same weekend across the city, a group of Huntington adults tried something almost as dangerous and brave -- spending the night at the Cincinnati Zoo & Botanical Garden with a wild pack of first and second graders.

Arranged by the obviously fearless and/or crazy Pack 21 Cub Scout leaders, Kari and Chris Newman back in the winter, the unique group overnight trip was part of the Zoo's Nocturnal Adventures Program.

That decades-old program lets chaperoned groups spend the night at the zoo for what's billed as "the wildest nightlife in town," well, at least on that end of Vine Street.

Designed for critters ages eight and up and chaperones, the program has a wide range of options that lets older kids do overnights at Wolf Woods, while younger kids can Sleep With the Manatees or sleep in the Harold C. Schott Education Center, that is part of the Zoo's tropical conservatory.

Our crew dropped off sleeping bags and backpacks inside the Conservatory inhabited by such "wild" creatures as the Fruit Loops mascot, a toucan, and a sloth, that I think was really just a stuffed animal or just channeling his inner Webkins.

Thank God for small favors. I couldn't imagine the bedwetting by the dozens that would have went on if we'd had to stay with wolves howling just outside our sleeping bags. I mean, hey, I do get a little scared at night without the contacts in.

With seasoned pros like Julianna Johns and Devon Capella as our zoo guides, they outlined the program that started at 7 p.m., and then went overnight until 9 a.m., when you're set free to go explore the zoo on your own.

"Our first rule is respect for everybody," Capella said. "And when we go out, no cameras. The animals are chilling. They're movie stars all day long, and right now is prime time for them."

It certainly was for us, too.

Parents, scouts and siblings sat cross-legged on the floor while these gals -- long on humor and patience -- brought out three quirky animals including a Madagascar Hissing Cockroach, an African Pygmy Hedgehog and "Boccie," the big ball of armadillo energy that ran around in circles with those tiny legs while we all almost fell over laughing.

"She's a little like a wind-up toy," Johns said. "She just goes and goes in circles."

Sounding like some other wind-up critters seated nearby, the gals got this wild pack of wolf and tiger Cubs up and outside for a behind-the-scenes peek inside the Nocturnal House and the World of Insects.

With the sun setting as we walked over past the Cat House, we all saw why this was already so worth it.

While most big cats and many zoo animals spend summer days snoozing as the sun bakes down, the Siberian Lynx and the Snow Leopard were both out scrambling about on boulders with crowds gone and night falling.

Since Johns is an expert on insects, we got the full tour of the World of Insects, and no nosy grade-schooler questions could derail the flow of her fountain of knowledge.

"Are they stuck to each other?" asked little Jordan Merry,

pointing at a couple of uh, friendly beetles in the aquarium.

"Well, it's spring and they like to get close to each other," Johns said, without missing a beat.

Hmmm, I think I'll keep her on speed dial to help us with "the talk" here in a few years.

While we all got a chuckle at the cicada exhibit, we also marveled at the brilliant design of such insects as the sunburst diving beetle that carries a bubble of water with it underwater so it can breath, and which was the inspiration, Johns said, for the creation of SCUBA gear.

Slipping through the "authorized personnel only" door at the Nocturnal House, we got the full show-and-tell talk from Capella, including getting to see the big jug o' cow's blood kept in the fridge for the daily diet of the vampire bats. We later learned that they

don't actually suck blood (that's so Hollywood). They just drink blood.

Inside the Nocturnal House, we got to see the rare activity of the South American pygmy marmoset, which, at 4.7 inches long, is the smallest monkey in the world.

Think of a tiny intelligent, expressive face slightly smaller than a ping pong ball.

We didn't see this guy at all the next day with the zoo packed with people, but at night with the Nocturnal House lit up in black light and only the sound of the A/C running, this little guy was jumping about and enjoying life as best he can.

After a visit to the Cat House, we walked back for a snack and while Jake asked if it was '12 o'clock yet?' it was not. The evening still had a night-hike.

With closed eyes and hands locked on shoulders, an 11-Cub-Scout-centipede formed, then strolled through the grounds slowly, twisting through the zoo, mouths closed and ears open, listening intently for night sounds of animals.

Peacocks rustled in the distance, and parents stood amazed at the collective quiet.

"She's got a gift," Chris Newman said of Capella. "She's the child whisperer."

While you've got to be a good sport for the accommodations (see: sleeping bag on floor), it's that rare free flow of access and education without hordes of other people that makes the Nocturnal Adventure worth every cent of the $35 admission.

We woke Sunday morning, and after breakfast were treated to the Wings of Wonder bird show.

Although the zoo's summer bird show with 26 birds wasn't going to open for another day, we again got the rock star treatment as Eddie Annal and his lovely assistants, a spectacled owl, a kookaburra and a blue/gold macaw put on an amazing show for our little Cub Scout crew.

When the program let out at 9 a.m., it was still relatively cool, and the floods of folks were yet to come through the gates.

With the rest of the fam now on board and our good friends, Jill and Jamie Jones and their gals toddling along, we got to see more of the zoo and got to see it before the throngs and the heat began mixing that afternoon cocktail of annoyance.

When the clock struck 2 p.m., and overheated moms and dads started grinding teeth and drafting and bumping strollers in Manatee Springs like it was a NASCAR Sunday afternoon at Bristol, I knew it was time to take songwriter Don Schlitz's advice and know when to walk away and know when to run.

Making a great escape as people were still pouring into the zoo, this father felt grateful to spend such a wonderful evening with my son and all the scouts and families, and to realize humbly that while we make up a pretty cool pack, we aren't even close to being the coolest animals on the planet.

Let's Go Trippin: Cincinnati Zoo

WHAT: The Cincinnati Zoo's overnight program, Nocturnal Adventures, for special evenings designed for parents and children, age 5 and up. During the program, you will hike the Zoo, go behind the scenes, experience live animal encounters, and engage in other exciting activities. Awake to peacock and gibbon calls, have breakfast, and then enjoy a special animal show. Family Overnight start at 6pm. Please arrive 15-20 minutes early.

HOW MUCH: $30/ Member, $35/ Non-Member

WHERE: Camp Out participants will sleep outside near the Education Center, behind the Giraffe Ridge exhibit. Sleep with the Manatees participants sleep in the Manatees Springs building. Most other family overnights sleep in the Harold C. Schott Education Center.

FOR MORE INFO: Questions? contact us at (513) 559-7767 or email registrars@cincinnatizoo.org

OTHER SLEEPOVER ADVENTURES: Newport Aquarium, in Newport, Ky. (across from Cincinnati) has an Overnight Adventure Program allows groups to spend the night with the most exotic and interesting creatures. Your group will explore hidden treasures of the Aquarium and visit with unique animals from around the world before camping out among amazing sea life. Kids must be six to participate. The program has special nights for Boy Scouts, Girl Scouts, Home Schoolers, although any youth group can make a reservation. Go online at http://www.newportaquarium.com/Groups/School-Groups/Overnights.aspx for more info.

COLUMBUS ZOO OVERNIGHTS: The Columbus Zoo has eight different overnight adventures. Community groups, and schools can opportunity to explore the Zoo when it is less crowded, experience up-close encounters with animal ambassadors, and see what the animals do after-hours all while learning about conservation and our natural world. Topics vary by grade level and are aligned with Ohio Academic Standards. For questions, call 614-645-3488 or camp.in@columbuszoo.org. A minimum of a three-week advance reservation is required. Minimum group size is 15. Cost is $35 with a $100 deposit for each room reserved.

Ohio

TECUMSEH OUTDOOR DRAMA

With school running into June and saddling back up in early August, summer increasingly gets squeezed.

And what with all the video game and "Dr. Who" watching marathons around the Lavender household, summer camps and not to mention the week-long no-power, Derecho-induced real-life "Survivor" episodes at our house, it has been lean times for planning a good old-fashioned jump-in-the-car Dave Trippin' with the family.

However, recently the road and duty called. My old biker blues band Haywire Dog (of which I was a member of in what seems like a time long, long ago in a galaxy far, far away) was gathering up for a reunion up in Chillicothe and playing a blues and jazz festival in Columbus.

I knew this was a great chance to load up the Dave Trippin' mobile (now a Mazda 5 - mini-mini-van) with more camping gear than should be legal and treat the boys to an amazing slice of our area's living history.

And I'm not just talking about the epic party, The Mustache Bash that the Chillicothe Elks threw for our old biker crew (Stoneface, Little Elvis, Jug, Ray, Jersey Bob, Little Jim, and Buckets and so many more), and of course, the band' stuffed Chihuahua, "Skippy."

Armed with our fresh fake mustaches from the "Stache Bash," the Lavender crew made its way over to Sugarloaf Mountain Amphitheater that's been literally blowing up theater nightly every summer for the past 40 years with the cannons-blasting, hair-raising, historical drama, "Tecumseh."

Written by the late, Emmy Award-winning writer Allan Eckert (whose books are still published by the Ashland-based Jesse Stuart Foundation), "Tecumseh" is I think for its scope and influence, perhaps Eckert's greatest living legacy.

But don't just take my word for it, as the numbers do not lie.

More than 2.5 million people have made their way to Chillicothe since Eckert and original producer Rusty Mundell and the Scioto Society birthed "Tecumseh."

Led this year by Trindad native Stevyn Carmona, who is the 19th actor to play the great Shawnee leader, "Tecumseh" is being performed Mondays through Saturdays through Labor Day weekend in Chillicothe, which is about two hours straight north of Huntington in south-central Ohio.

For folks who slept through history class and know only that the War of 1812 was fought in 1812, "Tecumseh" tells the life story of the legendary Shawnee leader from the late 1700s and through his death in 1813 as he struggles to defend his people's sacred homelands in the Scioto and Ohio River valley.

As American pioneers continued to push west over the Allegheny and Appalachian mountains encroaching on his home, Tecumseh tries against all odds to rally all of the very different and often warring Native American tribes in the region as one, teaming with the British (still stinging from the Revolution) against the American pioneers who after receiving land grants from fighting in the Revolutionary War were aggressively advancing westward to settle.

Like Jenny Wiley Theatre in Prestonsburg, Ky., and Theatre West Virginia in Grandview, W.Va. (near Beckley), "Tecumseh" has a legacy of entertaining and (don't tell the kids) but slipping in more than a little bit of regional history education into their summer.

No one captured the daily chaos and influential moments of the founding of our frontier nation more vividly than Eckert, the seven-time Pulitzer Prize-nominated Buckeye native whose legacy in print includes the "Winning of America" series and "A Sorrow in Our Heart: The Life of Tecumseh," from which the outdoor drama is carved.

It is a worthy task to lay into one of Eckert's Bible-length "Winning of America" works about the struggles between the Native Americans and the crazy quilt of American pioneers, British, French and other traders who all laid claim to the rich and fertile Ohio River Valley land that was already occupied. Diving into that series is also quite an unrealistic task for most tweens already spellbound with one Harry Potter.

Thus "Tecumseh" with its poignant, fast-paced script written by Eckert, and its action-packed cast of more than 100, is the perfect gateway history drug for curious kids wanting to dive deeper into the rich Native and pioneer history that lies just under the surface here in our hills and river bottoms.

A big part of the magic of "Tecumseh" is that you are in the set. The outside aisles of this drama feel the breeze of horses galloping and snorting just feet away as they tear down sandy paths toward the bottom of the main set flanked by two large rock cliffs with multiple levels and that is in front of a large pond that leads deeper into and open backdrop of woods.

The actors are so close you almost expect them to stop by for a Twizzler, and you are surrounded by a superb sound system that booms with the God-like voice of narrator Academy Award-nominated Graham Greene, as well as the Carl Fischer-written score recorded by the London Symphony Orchestra.

Although the actors don't interact with you, they are so close that the musket and cannon firing can scare the daylights out of little kids who get easily blurred lines about reality and theater. It's stated that the show is not for anyone ages 6 and under or kids, I would say, who are sensitive to really loud noises.

If they are, it's best to try and sit in the back or the middle of the amphitheater.

Also, if you have time, get there as the cast does an amazing backstage tour at 4 p.m. and 5 p.m. during which you can learn how hardy veterans such as Raymond Speakman (in his 30th year with "Tecumseh") puts together the pyrotechnics and the stage fighting (that includes actors falling off a 21-foot-high cliff).

If you want to make a weekend of it, there are several nearby state parks for camping, including Great Seal State Park which is literally next door to the property. There's also a 30-mile-long rails-to-trail, canoeing on Paint Creek, and everyone should try to visit one of our closest National Park units, Hopewell Culture National Historical Park to learn even more about the ancient native history of the Moundbuilders.

Like many landmark experiences from our youth - whether it is Camden Park, Carter Caves, a classic drive-in like Stewarts or Frostop - you pray it's still brushed with the evergreen wonder for another generation.

At least for Toril and I and our two history-loving lads (ages 9 and 12) that certainly was the case for their first experience with "Tecumseh" as a Monday night was more than all right for horses-swimming, stage-fighting, and a moon, history and memories all a rising in the Shawnee's main town of Chillicothe.

Let's Go Trippin: Tecumseh

WHAT: "Tecumseh" Outdoor Drama

WHERE: Sugarloaf Mountain Amphitheater is located about two hours north of Huntington and just north of Chillicothe, Ohio (which is south of Columbus).

WHEN: At 8 p.m. Mondays through Saturdays, early June through Labor Day weekend

HOW MUCH: $25 and $15 (for kids 10 and younger). Not recommended for children ages 6 and younger due to some violent content and loud battle scenes.

GET TIX: Reservations can be made online at www.tecumsehdrama.com or by calling 1-866-775-0700

WHAT ELSE AT TECUMSEH: Get there early for backstage tours, there's also a museum and a restaurant on site. Also, check the schedule for off-day shows as well including bluegrass acts, and other theatrical presentations.

GETTING THERE: Take U.S. 52 west to Portsmouth to U.S. 23 north. Or take Route 2 out of Huntington to Point Pleasant and then U.S. 35 (over the bridge in Gallipolis, Ohio) all the way to U.S. 23 and Chillicothe. From Chillicothe take the exit just north of downtown that says "Outdoor Drama" and follow the signs.

WHAT ELSE IN CHILLI: Go online at www.visitchillicotheohio.com for a complete list of cool places to visit. Don't miss the free NPS site, Hopewell National Historic Park.

COOL EATS: Kick it old-school at some of these Chilli favorites; Sumburger Drive-In, Carl's Townhouse, The Cozy Inn, The Crosskeys Tavern and Jerry's Pizza.

CAMPING NEARBY: You can practically throw a rock from "Tecumseh" and hit Great Seal State Park that has 15 camp sites (non-electric). There's a disc golf course there too and good hiking trails. Go online at http://parks.ohiodnr.gov/greatseal

More Outdoor Theater

Here's a look at some more outdoor theater in the region:

HART In The Park: Huntington Area Regional Theatre began in 2014 partnering with the Greater Huntington Park and Recreation District to carry on the work of HOT or Huntington Outdoor Theater which ended its 20-year run in 2013. HART in the Park produces two summer shows at the Ritter Park Amphitheater as well as two children's pre-shows. The 2015 shows are the Clint McElroy/Danny Craig written original musical, "Collis P" and "Mary Poppins." Go online at www.ghprd.org for more info.

Theatre West Virginia: Located at Grandview in Beckley, W.Va., in the heart of the New River Gorge since 1955. Enjoy the historic "Hatfields and McCoys" and other shows in summer. Go online at http://theatrewestvirginia.com/ for more info.

The Aracoma Story: Select summer dates at the Liz Spurlock Amphitheater at Chief Logan State Park, Logan, W.Va. Based on historical facts and local legend, the drama unfolds as a wise old mountain man weaves the tragic tale of Aracoma, daughter of Shawnee Chief Cornstalk, and her ill-fated love for Boling Baker, a British soldier captured by her father. Call 304-752-0253 or visit visit http://www.thearacomastory.com.

Jenny Wiley Theatre: At Jenny Wiley Amphitheater at Jenny Wiley Resort State Park near Prestonsburg, Kentucky. Celebrated its 50th year in 2014, the summer stock theater has multiple shows in summer and expanded to year round shows in Pikeville. JWT has helped many professional actors cut their teeth on stage. Call 1-877-CALL-JWT or go online at www.jwtheatre.com.

Stephen Foster The Musical: Located at My Old Kentucky Home State Park in Bardstown, Ky., it tells the story of one of Kentucky's most famous composers ("Oh Susanna,' "Beautiful Dreamer," and "My Old Kentucky Home." The outdoor show celebrated its 50th year in 2008. Call 1-80-626-1563 or visit www.stephenfoster.com for more info.

Ohio

GREAT WOLF LODGE

Walking down the hallway at Great Wolf Lodge with the boys last weekend, I stopped and savored the rare winter sound -- the clip-clop of flip-flops.

Ahhhh. Like an echo off a distant sun-drenched canyon, that soothing sound of summer calling was just what we needed.

With another menacing blob of snow ready to blanket the Tri-State, the Dave Trippin' crew loaded up the swimsuits and headed west to Cincinnati to take February out like a Great Wolf.

While West Virginia is blessed with great skiing with five downhill resorts, and while Kentucky has a world to be found underground in the great caves from Mammoth Cave to Carter Caves, the winter-whipped Buckeye State has taken a cue from Buckeye Chuck (the state groundhog) and has burrowed inside.

In the past few years, Ohio has built a waterpark wonderland with eight indoor waterparks near the amusement park meccas of Sandusky and Cincinnati as well as Columbus.

One of the largest and closest to the Tri-State is **Great Wolf Lodge** (www.greatwolf.com) that sits like a giant Lincoln-log-looking fortress of fun perched within view of the giant coasters of Kings Island in Mason, Ohio (just north of Cincinnati).

Like a Peter Pan-designed hotel, Great Wolf, opened in late 2006, is a seemingly never-ending neverland of fun with its main attraction -- Bear Track Landing, a 79,000-square-foot water park featuring a dozen waterslides, six pools and a four-story treehouse waterfort.

When we rolled up to the Great Wolf (about a three-hour drive from Huntington) we immediately felt right at home.

Nice to see that the Lavenders aren't the only ones still sporting

a little Christmas decoration as the giant log structure was still adorned with three giant Christmas wreaths.

Frankly, we didn't care if the Halloween decorations were still up, after weeks of frosty temps we were taking the sage advice of fellow Huntingtonian, Vince Hebert, who had just got back from the lodge with his two kids -- "Drive to Great Wolf, park your car, and don't go back outside."

Heeding Hebert's advice we ventured into the North Woods-themed family resort home to 401 all-suite guest rooms, a full-service spa, fitness center, themed restaurants and a 7,000 square-foot arcade in addition to the water park.

With another snowstorm turning the parking lot's cars into what looked like a bag of marshmallows below, and with the temperatures staying below 20, we didn't go outside for two days.

Although the kids-themed rooms are pretty amazing (kids bunk down in cave, wolf den or kids cabin theme rooms), there's a ton of activities that keep the kids constantly roaming the hallways of this magical, mystical lodge.

Before we even made it inside the waterpark, the kids discovered MagiQuest, one of the world's first live action fantasy adventure games that is played inside the hotel's mural-painted hallways divided into such areas as Whispering Woods.

Set up throughout the hallways and lobbies of the third and fourth floors, MagiQuest lets kids get in touch with their inner Harry Potter, using wands to tromp around on various quests, opening treasure chests along the way, talking to trees and fairies, lighting up crystals and battling ogres and dragons.

During this last weekend of the Olympics, it gave new meaning to the phrase "going for gold" as we logged hours and probably dozens of miles going up and down the staircases trying to keep up with our wild little wizards in training, who woke up at the crack of dawn to begin the Quest again.

A tip for those going to Great Wolf, it's dang near impossible to resist the temptation of the quest, so on advice from Vince we got a Paw Pass for the kids to share.

Although an extra $60, the Paw Pass allowed the kids to play the MagiQuest all weekend, get tokens for the arcade, as well as

decorate a T-shirt and pillowcase, stuff an animal to take home, and get a giant drink and souvenir cup in the water park.

For wee tots, the lodge's Grand Lobby has a sweet animatronic musical show with a little boy Simon, his Indian friend, Yellow Feather, and a chorus of singing moose, squirrels and other critters that takes place in front of the giant three-story clock tower, whose time is told by two giant feathers.

Top that off with the arcade, unique restaurants like the Camp Critter Bar and Grille, where the fam can eat inside a booth

enclosed by a tent, you could arguably not even hit the waterpark and have a great time.

For waterdogs of all ages, Bear Track Landing, the indoor water park, is an amazing place to splash down.

Open 10 a.m. to 8 p.m. Sunday through Thursday and 10 a.m. to 10 p.m. on the weekends, you can get in more water play than an otter in the park's 12 water slides that includes the new one-of-a-kind five-story waterslide, the Triple Twist (which was scheduled to open March 4), as well as a water roller coaster ride, a cannon bowl tube, three tube slides and a couple body slides.

Not unlike its summer-time neighbor King's Island, the sheer size of the water park is impressive and can be overwhelming. There are six pools, including a nice lazy river, a wave pool, a zero-depth entry (for wee tots), a family whirlpool and an adult whirlpool at Great Wolf, which now has 13 sites in the U.S. and Canada including one in Sandusky, Ohio, as well by Cedar Point.

One of the boys' favorite things was Fort MacKenzie, an interactive treehouse waterfort that featured dozens of water buckets, squirtguns, pipes that created a constant sprayground of fun. At the top, there were two smaller water slides for kids of all ages, and on the roof of Fort MacKenzie, the 1,000-gallon water bucket that was perpetually filled and dumped.

One of the great thing about Great Wolf is that adults sure haven't been left out in the cold, so to speak.

Opened in 2006, and one of a dozen Great Wolfs across North America, the lodge in Mason, has thought of it all from Grizzly Rob's tiki bar inside the waterpark to extra steps of convenience. For instance, a plastic wristband served as room key, waterpark admission and credit card for the weekend -- no going to a locker or rummaging through backpacks for always soggy dollars to buy an ice cream or drink at the pool.

That said, folks do have to realize that while the bands are so easy to use, and although goods inside are moderately priced (they had an $8.95 extra-large pizza) you can rack up a higher bill than Tiger Woods at a beauty pageant if you don't keep track of spending.

For families watching the budget (and who isn't?) the rooms come with good-sized refrigerators and microwaves so that you can cook some of your meals in the room if you'd like.

Another nice touch at Great Wolf is that they're the one of the first national hotel chains to be Green Seal certified, and since the Lavenders are green, it felt like home. There were recycling bins around the lodge, as well as in the room, low-flow showers, and a recirculation system in the pool that recycles most of the water.

The Lavender boys could have stayed at Great Wolf forever, but Sunday morning was coming down. The bill was slipped under the door and -- although you can stay at the waterpark for the

whole day on your check-out day -- we were happily wiped out and water-logged. It was time to boogie back to the Tri-State.

Before we left Cincy, though, we couldn't resist a few more gallons of fun. OK, a million more gallons of fun.

We trucked over to the Southern Side of Cincinnati, and the Newport Aquarium, which like our oldest son Jake, is also turning 10.

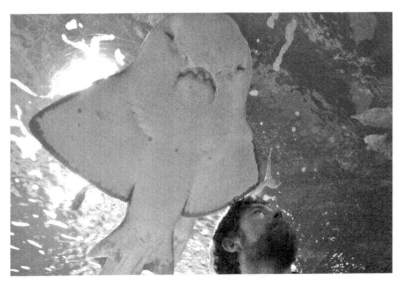

Located on the banks of the Ohio River in the Newport on the Levee development, **Newport Aquarium** (www.newportquarium.com) was a wonderful winter stop where we spent hours staring at colorful worlds of tropical fish, jellyfish, sharks and the unique shark rays located in the aquarium's more than 70 exhibits and 14 galleries.

Luckily, we stopped by on the last day of the Aquarium's deal that two kids get in with one adult, so we all got in for about $44.

Before we could venture down the escalator and into the heart of the aquarium, we stood along with a hundred or so other folks who smashed together to see the Penguin Parade, during which three African penguins named, "Simon, Randy and Paula," (who knew they were still together) were rolled out across the red carpet entrance.

Then, as zoos and aquariums do so well, we found out in mere minutes more information than should be legal about those critters: Eight out of 18 penguin species live not in the Arctic but on the beach in warm climates, that they swim 16 miles an hour while Olympic swimming stud Michael Phelps swims eight mph, that these penguins can eat 40 fish a day, and that these little guys in the wild take a Nixon every 18 minutes then build a house out of their own scat.

Good Lord. Armed with way too much information and visuals about penguin lifestyles, we headed into the aquarium.

Not unlike the 10-year-old in our crew, the aquarium is still growing, and changing with several old exhibits being swapped out, and several of the new tunnel tanks being added.

We loved Frog Bog where kids could crawl through a play area that not only included a maze of tunnels and slides, but also little exhibits of frogs that only the kids could see from inside.

Like other regional aquariums such as Ripley's in the Smokey Mountains, Newport's calling card are the seamless see-through, acrylic tunnels.

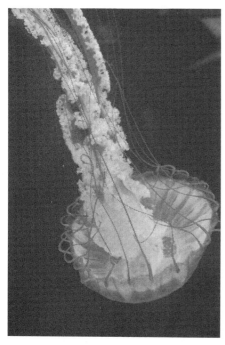

They've got five that total more than 200 feet in length and none more impressive than "Surrounded by Sharks," whose 85 feet of tunnels give you a unique window into this 385,000-gallon tank filled with up to 10-foot Sand Tiger sharks, as well as Sandbar, Whitetip Reef, Blacktip Reef, Nurse, and Zebra sharks all peacefully swimming with Southern Singrays, Honeycomb Whiptail Rays, reef fish, a giant Loggerhead Sea Turtle and the aquarium's two unique Shark Rays, Sweet Pea and Scooter.

Like any trip to this Aquarium, you've gotta make a couple long stops at the art gallery-esque, Jellyfish Gallery where you can sit in the cool and the dark on comfy seats and watch framed aquariums of jellies and the sea nettles thread their way through the water.

With a Sunday slipping away, and with images of water slides and jellyfish glides dancing in our heads we finally, went back outside, pulled the ol' swagger wagon onto the AA and headed home.

Like Will, our 7-year-old, had said when he came out of Great Wolf, "I forgot all about winter."

Yes, and for a little while, so did we.

Let's Go Trippin: Great Wolf Lodge

WHAT: Great Wolf Lodge, 2501 Great Wolf Drive, Mason, Ohio

WHERE: At Kings Island, in Mason, Ohio (just north of Cincinnati). About 156 miles from downtown Huntington.

WET AND WILD: Great Wolf Lodge has a 93,000-square-foot indoor entertainment area that features one of the country's largest indoor water parks, Bear Track Landing. The 79,000-square-foot park has 12 waterslides: Two body slides, three tube slides, four kiddie, the new water roller coaster ride, cannon bowl tube ride and raft ride. The Triple Twist is a five-story waterslide featuring a drop into a huge funnel followed by twists and turns and two more funnels. And at night, The Triple Twist takes it up a notch as you are immersed in a full-sensory LED lighting experience. There's also six pools (including a wave pool), an interactive treehouse waterfort with a 1,000-gallon tipping water bucket.

WHAT ELSE: The water park also has a snack bar, swim shop, airbrush tattoo stand and Grizzly Rob's bar.

ALSO @ THE LODGE: There's also Elements Spa Salon, the Scoops Kid Spa, the Cub Club (for daily crafts and storytime), IronHorse Fitness Center, a conference center and MagiQuest, the first live action fantasy adventure game, inside the hotel.

GOOD EATS: Great Wolf Lodge is packed with restaurants including Loose Moose Cottage (serves buffet breakfast, lunch and dinner), the Camp Critter Bar and Grille, Pizza Hut Express, Starbucks, and Bear Paw Sweets and Eats.

MORE INFO: Go online at www.greatwolf.com.

GOOD STUFF NEARBY: Cincy is packed with great stuff for kids including the Cincinnati Museum Center at Union Terminal, the Cincinnati Zoo, King's Island, Jungle Jim's International Market, Ozone Zipline Adventure, and also, the Newport Aquarium, just over the Ohio River in Newport. You can go online at http://www.greatwolf.com/mason/amenities/areaattractions to see a full range of nearby attractions at this resort tucked between Cincinnati and Dayton.

More Ohio Indoor Waterparks

With eight parks throughout Ohio offering unique combinations of waterslides, water rides, pools, and full-service spas. Here's a look at those parks:

Castaway Bay at Cedar Point in Sandusky: Castaway Bay features 237 hotel rooms and suites including family-oriented units, a 38,000-square-foot indoor waterpark loaded with water activities for all ages, a day spa, fitness center, 6,000-square-foot arcade, a craft and child activity center and three restaurants. Go online at www.castawaybay.com

CoCo Key Water Resort at Cherry Valley Lodge in Newark :This 50,000-square-foot waterpark east of Columbus, eatures a décor and at Cherry Valley Lodge the park also includes

an indoor/outdoor spa, activity pool with basketball hoops, raft waterslides, arcade, snack bar, lounge, and cabanas. Go online at www.cherryvalleylodge.com/coco-key/

Fort Rapids Indoor Water Park in Columbus: This western-themed watermark features 12 water slides, a 1,000 gallon tipping bucket, gliding down the Cowboy Creek Lazy River or soaking in the 30-person hot tub. Fort Rapids offers 277 tower guest rooms and 60 villa family suites. Go online at www.fortrapids.com

Great Wolf Lodge in Sandusky: An enormous north woods-themed waterpark includes eight water slides, five pools – indoor recreation pool, zero-depth entry children's pool, giant water fort and a leisure river; and two whirlpools - family and adult. Go online at www.greatwolf.com/sandusky/waterpark

Kalahari Resort in Sandusky: One of America's largest indoor waterparks with 80,000-square-feet of African-inspired excitement. In addition to the slides and the Zip Coaster uphill roller coaster slide, the resort features nearly 900 African-themed guest rooms and suites, a fitness center, spa, shopping and dining. Go online at www.kalahariresorts.com/oh/

Splash Harbor in Bellville: (south of Mansfield on I-71) is a 6,000-square-foot tropical-themed atrium, with retractable roof. IT has a 49-foot looping water slide, water spray area, a large swimming pool with two basketball hoops; and a kiddie pool area. Go online at www.splashharbor.com

Rainwater Park in Sandusky: Rain indoor waterpark offers thrill slides and water play, featuring a 50-foot tower with two giant slides (each more than 250 feet long). There is a play structure with additional water activities and an outdoor pool. As the name indicates, waterpark guests are frequently showered with rain. Go online at www.rainwaterpark.com

CoCo Key Water Resort: Crowne Plaza Cincinnati North Cincinnati is a 50,000-square-foot indoor water park with four story water slides, lazy river, buckets that dump several gallons of water every few seconds and more fun-filled water activities. There also are exciting arcade games, birthday party rooms and more. Go online at www.cocokeycincinnati.com

Florida

FLORIDA KEYS

Finally the sun has shone, dandelions have popped up onto shaggy green lawns and West Virginia's ski resorts have not had to announce they are extending the season into July.

It was only weeks ago though when skies were smeared with black and gray, and cantankerous morning clouds coughed up endless snow and cold and misery.

With spring having a harder time starting than a 1978 Ford Pinto, the Dave Trippin' crew could take it no more -- we broke the emergency glass and reached for four cheap tickets to paradise for a much-needed Spring Break getaway.

Thanks to those cheap and easy two-hour direct flights to Fort Lauderdale (www2.allegiantair.com/) Tri-Staters can be roaming the wilds of Southern Florida faster than we can be watching those million dollar thoroughbreds run over at Lexington's Keeneland Race Course.

And as we found out, if you're not eaten by gators in the Everglades or carjacked in Miami, you can be sitting way down in the heart of the Florida Keys in as much time as it takes to drive to Cleveland.

Since we were meeting up with a slew of family a day later, we rented a car in Fort Lauderdale and popped down to Florida City/ Homestead, located just east of Miami and just a stone's throw from the Everglades.

Since I've been a lifelong sucker for roadside attractions such as our beloved Mystery Hole and Ripley's Believe It or Not, our first stop was at **The Coral Castle** (28655 South Dixie Highway, Homestead, Fla.).

Often called America's Stonehenge, the inspirational Coral

Castle is the mind-blowing work of Edward Leedskalnin, a 100-pound Latvian immigrant who from 1920 to 1940 used his ingenuity, junkyard car parts, pulleys and the abundant coral to carve and place massive monuments to his life's love who would not marry him.

Pretty impressive since most of us only built beer can pyramids to our long gone teen angels.

Now oddly surrounded by strip malls and on a busy road, The Coral Castle was the site of Billy Idol's video, "Sweet Sixteen," which he wrote about the couple and the refreshingly odd world of coral that includes a 25-foot-tall 40,000 ton telescope, stone rocking chairs, a table carved in the shape of Florida, and of course, the three ton gate that the tiny builder could push open with his little finger.

While Miami is also just a quick shot east from Homestead/Florida City, we nature lovers turned our rental horseless carriage (both coming and going from the Keys) to the river of grass, the Everglades National Park, only 11 miles away from Homestead.

With strawberry season just on in vast farm fields we twice had to hit the epic fruit stand, **"Robert Is Here,"** (www.robertishere.com) where Robert Moehling (who checked us out) has been running this super-sized stand since 1959 -- when he was 6-years-old and convinced his pops to let him sell their fruit.

Packed with fresh produce from the nearby fields and more than 30 kinds of tropical fruit, "Robert is Here" was a fam favorite.

Fueled up on their famed fruit shakes, we drove to the Royal Palm Visitor Center home to two drastically different trails.

After wrapping our rental car in tarps (Florida buzzards will literally eat every scrap of rubber, e.g. tires and windshield wipers), we popped onto the shady Gumbo-Limbo Trail for an easy 30-

minute hike through the canopy of hammock trees with their sprawling roots, royal palms and ferns a plenty.

On the other side of the visitor center, and just a few feet lower in elevation is the Everglades that is advertised. The Anhinga Trail, named for the fine-feathered local bird, snakes along the Taylor Slough on paved sidewalks and boardwalks packed with a near Disney-like amount of wildlife.

Just half a mile long, the boardwalk winds past more animals and birds than I've seen anywhere. It's dang near a gator convention that also happens to be attended by many herons, egrets, turtles and fish.

While we love a good canoe trip, seeing one too many gators and hearing about three too many python stories, we decided to let the pros do the "paddling" and by paddling we mean revving up an airboat to slip out into the heart of the Glades.

Taking the Shark Valley entrance (U.S. 41 which connects Miami and Naples), we motored over to the Miccosukee Indian Reservation for the **Buffalo Tiger's Everglades Boat Tours** (http:// buffalotigersflevergladesairboattours.com) where an older couple from England walked up to me (sporting my camo hat and my obvious need of a good haircut) in a huff and asked me what time the boat rides started.

While there's an airboat tour every mile or so on the old Tamiami Trail, we enjoyed this one driven by one of the young men of the tribe. In the tour, he drove us back some 3 1/2 miles into the Everglades, pulled up some of the sawgrass for us to taste the roots that the Miccosukee would eat, would call in the birds and called a gator over to the boat as well. The trip also took us back to a traditional Indian camp on a tiny island (filled with very, very squishy soil) where we gingerly walked around before being blasted back through the mud and the grass.

While we could have easily bummed around Miami and the Glades for a week, with a family full of writers, we were anxious to get to down into the Keys where Ernest Hemingway and Zane Grey would go to write, hang out and hide out.

It is 106 miles from Key Largo (at the top of the Florida Keys) to Key West and from Key Largo's Christ of the Deep (the 9-foot-state of Jesus sank into the waters of John Pennecamp Coral Reef State Park) to Key West's slew of watering holes like Sloppy Joes and the sunsets at Mallory Square. There isn't hardly an inch of those islands that is not off the charts interesting.

Supporting our sister-in-law (a mama-to-be and editor at Fodor's) we went armed with their new pocket-sized "Florida Keys" planner that helped us find some awesome family-friendly joints, such as **The Hungry Tarpon at Robbie's Marina** (www.hungrytarpon.com) and educational outings, such as the incredibly fascinating, **Turtle Hospital** in Marathon, Fla. (www.turtlehospital.org).

The drive down through the Keys -- in particular the famous 7-Mile-Bridge -- was one that noticeably lifted all spirits. Mile by mile our eyes were awash in eight shades of blue and green as we made our way down to Big Pine Key surrounded only it seemed by shallow sea and sky.

While we had two sets of friends friends from Huntington staying on other keys (the rowdier and more historic Key West and the also bustling Islamadora in the Upper Keys), we, rolling with a more outdoorsy crew and even a scientist on board (picture Gen. Robert E. Lee armed with a microscope and insect net) stowed away on Big Pine Key, which is called the natural key. It is home to the **National Key Deer Refuge,** a 84,824-acre refuge that is the hangout to the tiny-legged Key Deer, the runt cousin of the whitetail deer we all know, love and hate here in West Virginia.

Offered up instead of Christmas and birthday gifts, my wife Toril's folks graciously got a week rental house for us and her brothers. Like a tropical postcard, the house's back lawn of sand and palms was located across the bridge and bay from **Bahia Honda State Park** (36850 Overseas Highway). Bahia Honda is home to what Fodor's calls "the Keys' best white sand beach," the remains of Henry Flagler's railroad bridge (that once linked to Key

West) and home to great snorkeling and swimming since unlike most of the Keys, it's home to some deeper waters right off-shore.

Unfortunately, it's also home to plenty of dangerous wildlife too as my brother-in-law Aaron's foot found the working end of a surely Confederate stingray who did not seem to take too kindly to Yankee tourists rolling in from the Jersey shore. Howling, rightfully so like a house full of Hemingway's six-toed cats, Aaron toughed out stitches and soaking his foot in near boiling water (yes, that's the recommendation for stingray stings). A few medicinal brews and a couple days later, he was snorkeling with his foot wrapped in gauze and duct tape.

Thanks to Bill Keogh, a longtime Big Pine Key resident and author of "The Florida Keys Paddling Guide," we rented two double sea kayaks for the week for the price of one guided trip (www.keyskayaktours.com). It was great to be able to slide them into the water a couple times everyday for sunset paddles (where we saw a shark feeding just feet from our boats) and for exploration of the mangrove-rooted islands where schools of fish, rays and horseshoe crabs slid beneath the boat in the see-through shallow water.

Although our lily white red-headed freckle-faced crew had to slather on enough 100 spf sunscreen for an army, it was hard not to overindulge in this strange orange orb shining like a crazy diamond.

Since I always think it's fun to prep way in advance for a trip, we'd been swimming the boys all through the winter months at the YMCA with the neighbors each Wednesday (swimsday). So when we were in what is often called the Diving and Snorkeling Capital of the States, everyone in the fam got on board with **Strike Zone Charters** (www.strikezonecharters.com) for a snorkeling day trip ($35 a piece) out to Looe Key Reef, which is part of the expansive Florida Reef Tract that runs 358 miles off the Keys coast from the Dry Tortugas National Park off of the Florida Keys to the St. Lucie Inlet in Martin County.

It's a good thing we'd built up some strong swim strokes, even though it was relatively calm, waves crashed high over us as we

fought into the current (all swallowing our year's allotment of sea water) to look down into the color-splashed fish frenzy below -- everything from rainbow, midnight and blue parrotfish to large predators including a school of Great Barracuda prowling the reef.

We had a great time chilling on the quiet side of the Keys in Big Pine Key, whose only night spot is the famed 1936-built **No Name Pub** (www.nonamepub.com), and whose wallpaper is $75,000 in one dollar bills. But by mid-week we figured we should roll down to the tourist Mecca of Key West, and the Conch Republic that's been luring in the "unusual suspects" since the 1800s.

With three generations of folks walking through the Old Town with us, we smartly took two cars so that after a long day some of the fam could roll back, then others could stay to see a slice of Key West's legendary nightlife that begins each sunset with the human

carnival at Mallory Square and Pier. It is probably one of the few places where you can see a sunset and a full moon (about 20 folks on a sunset sail dropping drawers on us tourists gathered on the pier).

Meeting up with one of my son Jake's friends from Huntington Middle School, we watched some mind-boggling circus sideshow madness from sword swallowers and acrobats to a salty and hilarious British street magician whose final act was pulling a series of oranges out of a tiny bowler hat he'd been wearing the entire act.

With never-waning long lines at the Hemingway house, we let the boys pick a museum to ramble through and dove into the **Mel Fisher Maritime Museum** (www.melfisher.com) that tells of Fisher's quest to dive for the 1622-shipwrecked treasure-laden Spanish galleons.

We really dug the museum which not only had such stunning artifacts as the 77.76-carat emerald crystal, but also had a neat Harry Potter exhibit as well as a moving exhibit of the excavated 17th century slave ship, The Henrietta Marie that featured parts of the ship as well as such things as the iron bars they used to actually trade for human beings.

Thanks to a suggestion by the Tuckers, a Key West-loving couple from Proctorville, Ohio we met on the plane ride down, we noshed at the funky, junkyard-chic **B.O.'s Fish Wagon** (www.boswfishwagon.com) that they rightfully described as the

Hillbilly Hotdogs of Key West. Also on their recommendation, we had a neat visit to the secret tropical courtyard (where Hemingway stayed when he was first in the city) tucked inside the art and gift shop, the Pelican Poop Shoppe. I'm pretty sure we would have never found that.

Gliding back down at Tri-State Airport with skies still spitting cold and snow, we were glad to be back home, miraculously not sunburned and carrying back only memories of a Spring Break that was just what the doctor ordered.

With cheap direct flights from the Tri-State down into the heart of South Florida and a fam on board for new adventures beyond Orlando's mighty kingdom, here's hoping that we've all only yet begun to explore the Keys.

Let's Go Trippin: The Keys

WHAT: With cheap flights to South Florida out of Huntington and Charleston, there's quick access to the Florida Keys and The Everglades, two unique and fun family destinations., perfect for Spring Break trips.

GETTING THERE: While the Fort Lauderdale flight is gone from Tri-State airport, there still is Allegiant Air service to Fort Myers/Punta Gorda. It's a 3-hour, 20-minute drive along Route 41 that cuts through the heart of the Everglades (the largest remaining subtropical wilderness in the continental U.S.) to get to the top of the keys and the famous Key Largo. You can also take a water route, the boat shuttle between Fort Myers and Key West (www.fortmyerstours.com). Cost is about $95 each roundtrip.

THE GLADES: Cost is $10 per vehicle for a seven-day permit to explore the Everglades National Park. There's four main visitor centers from which you can plan a wide range of activities from hiking and bicycling to airboat tours and canoe trips.

DON'T MISS ROBERT IS HERE: Located at 19200 S. W. 344th St., in Florida City, Fla., is Robert Is Here. Birthed in 1960, the fresh fruit market has an incredible, fresh and wonderfully odd collection of fruit and produce and has fresh-fruit milk shakes that are amazing and a great healthy refuel for the road.

AN AIRBOAT RIDE: It's a ton of fun to walk the boardwalks into the Everglades, but nothing beats the experience of heading out into the wilds of the glades on an airboat. We took a rude with Buffalo Tiger's Everglades Boat Tours, located on (U.S. 41 that connects Naples to Miami. Go online at www.buffalotigerseverglladesairboattours.com

A GREAT GUIDE TO GET: At nearly 200 pages and pocket-sized the Fodor's Florida Keys guide from its In Focus series was incredibly helpful for pointing out the best places to eat, sightsee, and stay. Go online at www.fodors.com for more info

TOP OF THE KEYS TREATS: Fodor's Choice for eating near the top of the keys is the 1950s era floating barge, Alabama Jack's, 58000 Card Sound Road, located about 30 minutes from Key Largo. This well-weathered, floating restaurant is known for its live music and killer conch fritters and food at a great price.

Robbie's Marina: Located at 77522 Overseas Highway in Lower Matecumbe Key, Robbie's Marina, is a fun place for a fan to grab a bite to eat. The tourist draw is getting to hand feed the dozens of giant tarpons living the good life under the marina's docks. You can also shop a craft market here and catch a charter as well.

GREAT EDUCATIONAL STOP: The Turtle Hospital, located at 2396 Overseas Highway, is an awesome stop for families with kids interested in turtles and biology. Take a 90-minute tour to see more than 100 injured sea turtles all in various states of rehabilitation after being rescued from the sea. Cost is $15. Go online at www.turtlehospital.org

NOT TO MISS BEACH: Always ranked as one of the best beaches in the U.S., Bahia Honda State Park, located at 36850 Overseas Highway, has 2 1/2 miles of sandy beach, and snorkeling as well. There's a neat slice of history here too as the old Bahia Honda Bridge is part of what was Henry Flagler's railroad that once connected the keys before Highway 1. Go online at www.floridastateparks.org/bahiahonda

SNORKELING: The Keys are all about the water, and if you are a good swimmer you should try a snorkeling trip to one of the amazing reefs. At the top of the Keys, John Pennekamp Coral Reef State Park, U.S. Mile Marker 102.5 in Key Largo, is the top pick. Known as the first undersea park in the U.S., Pennekamp (named after the Miami newspaperman who helped establish the Everglades), the park encompasses more than 70 nautical miles and is known for it's snorkeling trips to see Christ of the Deep, a two-ton statue of Jesus. Go online at www.pennekamppark.com

LOOE KEY REEF: Known around the world for its Underwater Music Festival (the July fest where music is played underwater), Looe Key Reef is one of the Keys' most beautiful reefs with purple sea fans, elk horn coral and more. Trips run out of Ramrod Key and Big Pine Key. Go online at www.strikezonecharters.com for more info.

DRY TORTUGAS: In the Southern Keys, you can take a seaplane or ferry boat from Key West to the Dry Tortugas National Park, where you can tour the famous Fort Jefferson, picnic, bird watch and snorkel in this remote getaway some 70 miles off the coast Go online at www.nps.gov/drto

A NO NAME GETAWAY: Escape the crowds and catch a glimpse of the bizarre, Key Deer (the 30-inch tall white-tailed deer) during a stop at No Name Key. You can go to the National Key Deer Refuge, or just stop by the famous No Name Pub, (Mile Marker 30), on Big Pine Key, for a lunch at this funky former brothel and bait shop whose walls are decorated with dollar bills, and where the Key Deer congregate (in the parking lot) like cats at

Ernest Hemingway's house. Go online at www.nonamepub.com

IN KEY WEST: A really fun place to eat, which reminded us of Hillbilly Hotdogs, was B.O.'s Fish Wagon, 801 Caroline St., in Key West. It's funky and junky dining with no frills and all fun. Go online at www.bosfishwagon.com

MALLORY SQUARE: Don't miss a sunset at Mallory Square that's complete with spectacular views and a sideshow of street performers, magicians, jugglers, sword swallowers and the like.

MUSEUMS / GALLERIES: With kids, we didn't explore Key West's famous plethora of pubs, but it's also easy to wile away day or 10 at the collection of museums and galleries doting Key West from Ernest Hemingway's home and Mel Fisher's Maritime Museum to the good bargain of the Key West Museum of Art and History in the Custom House. Galleries showcase everything from famous photographers such as Alan Maltz to Cuban and Haitian art.

Florida

DISNEY

With our oldest son Jake soon heading off to the wild world of middle school next fall, I knew the clock was ticking toward D-Day, and boy was I dreading the requisite trip to Disney.

Seems that sometime soon after they passed the amendments to let someone other than well-heeled white men vote in the good ol' U.S.A, senators Lassie and Dick Van Dyke snuck in an amendment that if you're an American parent worth your Wheaties that some time in your child's raising you must haul 'em off to see Walt Disney World and revel in all of its joyous, gluttonous glory.

And like it, by golly.

So, although I'd rather have been on a slow train up Cass, W.Va., I found myself a few weeks back on spring break, hopping aboard one of those crazy-cheap direct flights to Florida (unfortunately well dubbed the OxyExpress) to do some Dave Trippin' to the planet of theme parks known as Disney.

While I left my street cred and wallet somewhere trampled by triple-kid-strollers on Magic Kingdom's Main Street, things were better than I feared. I seemed to have returned with at least part of my soul intact, and I sort of liked it.

Without further ado, here's Dave's dirty dozen (or less) tips for dads who gotta do the Disney.

Just Do It And Don't Wait

Setzer's World of Camping is right — "the kids are going to grow up and prices are going to go up." I love, love, love my parents who took us four snot-nosed brats to a million cool places but they hauled us to Appomattox Court House when I was about four (and knew more about the Dukes of Hazzard's Gen. Lee than

the real one), and then took us to Disney World when we were in high school. Yeah, backwards and awkwards. When two of my sisters and I were getting unmercifully pelted with "It's a Small World" singalongs our oldest sister was hosting her own version of "Space Mountain," — a week-long party back home with the parents in Fla. Ain't we got some sulky teenagers Griswold family fun!

So as soon as the kids are above the height to actually ride the real rides (about 44 inches for the parks and 48 inches for the water parks) and big enough to actually walk the 8 to 10 miles a day you'll be walking — bite the bullet and book it if you all like amusement parks.

Plan, Plan, Plan

Normally, the Dave Trippin' crew does a minimal amount of planning for trips so that the trail magic can just happen like stopping to stay all night at the Palace of Gold with the Hare Krishnas. Hey don't knock it until you've tried it.

But going to Disney isn't one of those let-it-just-happen trips. You really can't read and plan enough for a first trip. We planned for a good year. Email and get in the Disney system to get their DVD, planning guides and a PIN number for discounts. Scour books as the "Unofficial Guide to Disney" (very helpful) and talk to folks 'round here. Since Allegiant Air has been running non-stop, low-cost flights to Orlando since November 2006, there's folks here who've hit Disney more often than Lil' Wayne has hit a recording studio. We got lots of cost-saving tips (like www.mousesaver.com) from friends here in Huntington.

While we found a place (Pop Century) on the cheap inside Disney (less than $500 for seven nights), other folks we know here in H-town stayed at friend's condos in central Fla. for next to nothing.

Don't forget to shoot around a Facebook notice that you're planning a trip to see who may have a condo in the Orlando area.

And if you and the kids aren't in good physical shape, use the trip as a great excuse to get everyone practiced in walking and hiking daily — or at least a few times a week — to prep for a more pleasant trip.

When to Say When

Timing is everything and you can definitely avoid some of the worst crowds by not hitting peak weeks. This year the kids' spring break did not bump up against Easter which made it OK to go without a true crush of crowds. From Unofficial Guide, we got the "Lines" and "Tips" app which allowed us access to the year-round crowd calendar. On the web it's at (http://touringplans.com/walt-disney-world/crowd-calendar) where expected crowds are rated 1 to 10 with 10 being peak and stay the heck away.

Also, remember the temperature difference of central Florida. We went out of our cool, soggy cocoon of green here to the Palm tree grill of temps in the mid 90s in April. So if you're like our crew which tans about as well as a Maine lobster, June-July-August-September may not be your months.

There Is An App And A FastPass For That

Nobody likes to wait, and at Disney you really don't have to if you work the system right. We waited no more than 15 minutes for even the most popular rides thanks to Disney's FastPass system and to The Unofficial Guide to Disney's "Lines" app that lets you know how long the waits are for all of the parks' busiest rides.

The FastPass lets you use your ticket at the most popular rides to obtain one timed ticket per person. The FastPass gives you a designated time after which you can skip the regular line and zip right through the FastPass line to the front of the ride.

During the busiest days, it's worth designating someone to go nab FastPasses at the most popular rides and send another crew to go first thing and ride the most popular rides. We did that a couple mornings, nailing the largest rides early before the crushing crowds came.

Note the new policy is guests staying on Disney property can book up to three FastPasses per day ahead of time. After they use the initial three, they can obtain one more for the day for a total of four per day per person.

Exit Quickly Through the Gift Shop

Since Mickey Mouse has a Ph.D in emptying dad's wallets, you can't be unprepared since every ride ends in a gift shop stuffed with more versions of Mickey Mouse ears, pirate swords and cool merch than should be legal.

Knowing they'd be tempted at every turn, the boys got a budget of $50 which was chore-earned cash. We also brought a roll of pennies and quarters since every ride has a pressed penny or quarter souvenir machine to press coins with the image of the ride. A 51 cent souvenir? Sign me up and in your face Mickey Mouse.

Also for spending money, if you plan ahead, have grandparents bypass physical gifts for Christmas and birthdays and instead fork over some Disney gift cards to spend on food in the park. We got enough coin from the grayhaired set to pay for all meals at the park that we didn't pack in.

Got Groceries?

One nice thing on the cheap we did was hook up with Garden Grocer (www.gardengrocer.com). They deliver groceries to your hotel in Orlando, so when we arrived at our hotel room, they'd already filled it up with a week's worth of groceries that saved us hundreds of dollars.

You can pack in any food and beverages (no alcohol) to the Disney parks, and we took a backpack cooler to pack in wraps, healthy snacks and water bottles, which we refilled. Since the water in Disney parks is a bit different from our Ohio River vintage, we took lemonade packets to toss in. Just in water alone we figure we saved at least $80. Go online at (www.gardengrocer.com).

At least for us, but for many, Epcot Center is the most culinary interesting place as you can eat and drink (if you like $9 drinks) your way 'round the world. For meals in the park, it's definitely worth scouring the "Unofficial Guide" and other books that honestly, and sometimes brutally, rate all Disney restaurants. We found some inexpensive options with amazing outdoor spaces — a sweet little bonsai garden in Japan at Epcot, and a quiet lakeside shelter at Flame Tree Barbecue away from the raging crowds at Animal Kingdom.

Just Say No to Add-Ons

If you fly — and with these cheap flights and high gas nobody in their right mind would drive to Fla. — be sure to try and have the fam take one carry-on luggage (no bigger than 9-inches-by-14-width-by-22-inches deep) to forgo the $35 per person for checked

on baggage. Also, never pay for the long list of extras the airlines like to tag you with (like sitting together) and the same goes for Disney which has some pricey add-ons like Park Hopper.

Buy basic tickets

There's no reason to buy that upfront since you can add those on (park hopper and water parks) at the park (for the same price) if you would really like. Call me old-fashioned but it sounds a bit obsessive like one world-class amusement park in a day isn't enough. Like going to the Kentucky Derby downing juleps but being unsatisfied until you're whisked away to the Belmont Stakes.

Stay On Your Own Trip

With the hordes of jostling crowds and the pressure to "see it all" it's easy to get stressed, get ugly and go Clark Griswold on your crew. It's not necessary, and you don't have to "go" all the time. Make sure you take time to chill, nap and relax. When we were getting a bit frazzled and tired at Epcot, we pulled up on a grassy knoll and took a 30-minute nap. If we stayed late at a park one night, we rolled in late to another one the next day.

Be sure to know your family's routines. If you're early risers (and that pays off big time at the parks) get there before the park opens, and if you're staying on Disney property take advantage of the days you get can into selected parks even earlier than the general public or stay late.

If you're a late rising crew, get up casually, hit the pool and then go to the parks mid-afternoon.

Last but not least, be courteous, be kind but don't worry about everybody else there as you may very well encounter — like we did — every kind of crazy from chubby kids licking fallen desserts off the ground like they were on the set of "Willy Wonka" to moms going Mel Gibson-like nutso on crying toddlers at 11 at night.

Disney was right but so was John Prine. It may be a small world after all but it's big ol' goofy world too. And now thanks to direct flights we can easily trip to see Mickey, Goofy and friends then roll back to these sweet hilly arms of West Virginia in two hours — back to a real honest-to-goodness community with real people and real main streets filled with authentic potholes and everything.

Canada

PELEE ISLAND

Wolfe says you can't go home again.

Well, I've been back and I know that's true.

But you can thankfully go on vacation again, even if it now requires a passport card.

Often our vacation routes become deep furrows, fertile places, family vacation homes where we return and where memories stack up like the mish-mashed china and as comfy as the old furniture great uncle so-and-so drug out to the hunting or fishing cabin.

It has been rare for us to go to somewhere spectacular - put a good 20 years of time in between - and then actually get to return to that place.

But that happened a couple summers ago when we finally broke down and acquired passport cards which are much cheaper than regular passports but allow Americans limited travel to our neighbors who sandwich our States - Canada and Mexico.

With Toril's folks living in upstate New York, and us driving a couple times a year right past the exit ramp in Buffalo, N.Y., for Niagara Falls, Canada, we, of course, got to take the boys over the bridge and into the commercial vacationland of that Falls that Pigeon Forge-esque tourist wonderland full of bright lights and Ripley's Believe it or Nots.

While the boys had a ball exploring the roar and the refreshing fury of the falls (highly recommended off-season), Toril and I jonesed for the quiet and the island side of Canada that is - believe this or not - a doable weekend trip from Huntington. Don't tell anyone but awesome people but it's called Pelee Island.

In a 4 1/2 to 5-hour drive north you can be sitting in Sandusky, Ohio, home to Cedar Point (the roller coaster capital of the world), and the **New Sandusky Fish Company** (home to the best damn perch sandwich in the land).

OK, that's a long drive for a fish sandwich but that Fish Company, located at 235 E. Shoreline Dr., is just a couple blocks from the **Pelee Island Transportation Company** (1-800-661-2220) whose ferries, the MV Pelee Islander and MV Jiimaan ferry folks to Pelee Island from Sandusky to the south and Ontario to the north.

Located just a two-hour ferry ride from Sandusky, Ohio, the 16-square-mile Pelee Island (Ontario) is a true gem - a sparsely populated, and gorgeous destination for folks who want a quieter

getaway than such super popular and bar-packed Lake Erie destinations like Put-in-Bay, which rightfully deserves the "Key West of the Midwest" slogan, and which is can be an action-packed great lake escape if you're in a Jimmy Buffett frame of mind.

Toril and I first discovered the warm, and we do mean warm, embrace of the peaceful island back in the summer of 1995.

We were both working as cub photographer and reporter at the Chillicothe Gazette, in Ohio (just south of Columbus) and learned about the island (if we promised not to tell anyone else) from one of our good friends, Carl Hirsch, who in the wake of a divorce had found great solace in Pelee Island where pheasants and wine bottles, bicycles and gentle waves greatly outnumber the few people.

That summer of 1995, Toril and I had loaded up her 1992 Honda Civic (which is still operable to this day thanks to the alignment of two perfectly placed Mystery Hole bumper stickers) and raced north.

With temperatures soaring above 100 degrees we laughed about how smart we were to beat the heat only to find the temperature even on Lake Erie 100 degrees as well.

Although we think the temp got down to about 96 once we made the two-hour ferry ride to Pelee Island, and although we nearly

slapped each other silly thanks to welcoming parties of Canadian black flies and mosquitoes, we truly felt a world away. Worries melted away while floating out in our inflatable kayak in what felt like our own private Great Lake with barely another boat to be seen.

Both of us will never forget that trip. We were eating at one of the only restaurants on the island when a swift storm blew in and turned the sky and water into electric, vibrant colors with green water melting into eight shades of blue and into an angry black sky that tore through and took out the lights and electricity making for an impromptu candlelight dinner.

With those kinds of powerful memories forged in our heads we were anxious to take the kids who, at ages 11 and 8, seemed to question our sanity as to why we would get on a boat headed *away* from Cedar Point whose 20 roller coasters twist and curl along the Lake Erie shore calling their names to come and ride.

Will also seemed unimpressed by the collection of um vintage folks coming off the ferry from Pelee. "Is that a car show or an old man convention?" Will snapped as four antique cars rolled off the ferry boat after a weekend car show on the island.

Of course, as the seemingly endless panoramic temptation of Cedar Point faded away and was replaced by wind and waves, everyone's minds were swept away on a true journey forward into the deep endless blue of Lake Erie and its many islands.

While **Pelee Island** (www.pelee.org) does have a dozen bed and breakfasts, and three inns, we have long been the camping kind, and it is hard to imagine one more idyllic than **East Park Campground** (1362 East Shore Road) which has 25 wooded campsites, and a beach literally steps away across the road.

Will, who definitely in retrospect was in a bit of a snarky, straight-talk express phase, did question the music of some folky Canadians who'd maybe dipped a bit hard into the uh, Canadian Mist.

"Is that a mandolin?" I asked when I heard some music through the dark and through a grove of trees. "It's either a mandolin or a cat dying," Will dead-panned while Toril and I nearly fell into the fire laughing.

While the music wasn't exactly Appalachian Uprising campfire level and Gordon Lightfoot must have been camping elsewhere, the campground was cheap, breezy and easy. Going mid-week, we were able to practically have the beach to ourselves (and with our inflatable kayak) were able to explore along the shore. I must confess that with children we had too the added ease of playing in the freshwater waves and not being worried - like you can be along the saltwater beaches - that every sharp looking wave is a finned foe coming over to check out the fresh white meat buffet that is your frolicking family.

Although hearing we were headed to Lake Erie, our biologist friend Jeff Kovatch did remind us of a recent report of a lake snake infestation that we should be aware of.

While we tried to put the idea of giant leviathans of the deep coming for our toes out of our minds, we also figured we might check out some things on land, and to cast away some land fears as well.

Jake had only recently learned to really ride a bike and so we were excited to get him on a bike again and to try and pedal as much of the mostly agricultural island's interior, and to see as much of its shores as possible. We hooked up with **Comfortech Bicycle Rentals** (west dock, 1023 West Shore Road, 519-724-2828), where the boys each got bicycles (including the uniquely in-house designed Comfortech bikes) while Toril and I took on our own challenge - our

first ever attempt together on a tandem.

Let's just say no marriage has had a true test of merit until you've tried to pedal (and attempted to brake and stop) a bicycle built for two.

While we are pretty dang sure The Amazing Race is not going to

be calling us for our graceful glides, and seamless navigation, we did in our own slow and wobbly way soak in true adventure. On the way to the island's other side, we pedaled past mountain-sized piles of cut and discarded grapevine canes, and pedaled over to the north shore to enjoy exploring the trails to and around the 1833-built lighthouse where we gobbled a packed lunch and played again in the waves on what appeared at times during this midweek visit to be our own private island.

Although our time was limited, we figured that in the faith of our fathers, no trip anywhere was complete without carrying on the tradition of dragging the kids to a good history museum, and a good teachable amount among the artifacts and relics.

We found the **Pelee Island Heritage Centre** (073 West Shore Road, 519-724-2291) just a delightful reservoir of information about this odd little Southern Canadian island that the Centre reminds folks is home to everything from 20,000 pheasant, fields of vineyards, southern plants like the Prickly Pear Cactus and native Coffee trees and lots of history that comes to life in black and white photos of the hearty people who've ekked out a living in quarries and sawmills, steamships, ice boats and fisheries.

As someone whose ancestors are from the Commonwealth and who went to the University of Kentucky, one of the most interesting things I found out there was that perhaps the island's greatest attraction (Pelee Island Winery) was started by a Kentuckian (D.J. Williams) a Confederate sympathizer who fled to Canada to start the winery after the Civil War.

While we could have merely read all about it in Gary May's new book "Southern Exposure" (obviously not the same thing in

Canada as it is in Cabell County), we decided the only way to enjoy the history of **Pelee Island Winery** (519-724-2469) was to head over to the winery where new history is being made since the Winery sat defunct until 1979 when investors turned 600 acres of soybeans (which rumor has it make horrible wine), into grape vineyards.

Today, Pelee Island Winery is the largest estate winery in Canada. The day we went, even during the week, the winery was a buzz with activity, a full tour, a commercial being filmed of our tour, and lots of lively exchanges and food to be found (grill your own) at the Pavillion outside where the boys were able to eat their lunch up in a massive barrel.

With one last night left on the island, we loaded up the inflatable kayak and went to the beaches of the western side of the island.

We ate dinner down by the water, beachcombed until our eyes glazed over, and watched the orange ball melt into the great open lake.

With the sun and the boys' eyes setting, we took the car back to the campground to head to bed, but that would not happen for a while.

From a tranquil sun set in the west, the eastern side of the island

was channeling its inner Billy Idol with a full on rebel yell - a full moon rising, wind whipping up white-capped waves and creating such a magnetic fantastic energy that we found ourselves without discussion running into the water and time after time riding the waves in the boat into the black of the night.

While more distant shores of Maine (where Toril's grandparents have long had a family place) and comfortable Carolina beaches are more often in our vacation plans and on our radar, we found again, Pelee Island quietly calling, and we were so glad we answered the call for it was a true joy visiting this unique Southern slice of Canada, that can be, amazingly enough, enjoyed in just a weekend trip from Huntington.

Let's Go Trippin: Pelee Island

WHAT: Pelee Island is the largest island (10,000 acres) in the Western Basin of Lake Erie, in the Province of Ontario. It is located 122 miles from Sandusky, Ohio. There are 300 permanent residents and about 1,500 in the summer.

GETTING THERE: From May to September, you can catch the Ferry at Sandusky, Ohio. Go online at www.ontarioferries.com for more info. Call 1-800-661-02220 for more info.

STAYING THERE: Go online at www.pelee.org and check out links to about a dozen bed and breakfasts on the island as well as the East Park Campground which has 25 sites and the public East Beach just steps away. Cost is $20 per night for camping

WHAT TO DO: On Pelee, there is fishing and diving charters, a historic lighthouse, a heritage center, the Pelee Island Winery, restaurants and seasonal festivals.

EXPLORING THE ISLAND: Comfortech Bicycle Rentals 519-724-2828 and Explore Pelee Island (519) 325-8687 both have bicycle tours of the island. It takes about four hours to bike the island which has 34 kilometers of bicycle trails.

U.S. ISLANDS IN LAKE ERIE: If you don't have your passport card, go online at www.shoresandislands.com for tons of great info about Ohio's Lake Erie Shores and Islands.

Other Cool Boat Rides:

Here is a look at some other cool boat rides in the region:

The Belle of Cincinnati: BB Riverboats out of Newport, Ky., does an annual Ohio River trip stopping in cities such as Huntington, Ashland, Ironton, Maysville and Point Pleasant. Do not miss a summer trip on this great regional sternwheeler. Go online at www.bbriverboats.com for more info.

Blennerhassett Island: The history-rich island of Blennerhassett (between Belpre, Ohio and Parkersburg) is accessible seasonably by The Island Belle which takes visitors on a 20-minute boat ride to the historic-rich island and its mansion. The island can be explored by bicycle and other means. Go online at www.blennerhassettislandstatepark.com for the Belle's schedule and the schedule of special events on the island including the famed Mansion by Candlelight tour. Call 304-420-4800.

Whitewater Rafting: WV is home to the world famous New and Gauley rivers for whitewater rafting. Kids as young as 6 can ride the Upper New while those 12 and older can raft the Lower New River under the New River Gorge bridge. The Gauley River is a Top 10 whitewater river in the world, with more than 100 named rapids in 26 miles and is famous for its fall release. Check out the West Virginia Division of Tourism's whitewater web site at www.wvriversports.com

Hatfield and McCoys Airboat Tours: Run up the Tug River in an airboat (think Everglades tours) that roars up the river in Matewan in southern WV. Call 304-235-9090 for more info or go online at www.hatfieldmccouyairboattours.com

Summersville Lake: One of the deepest and clearest mountain lakes in WV known for its diving. and WV's only lighthouse. Boat rentals run the gamut from pontoon, fishing boats and kayaks to SUP (Standup Paddleboarding) run through area outfitters such as Adventures on the Gorge. Go online at www.summersvillelakeretreat.com for more info.

Cave Run Rentals: Over in Kentucky, the region's largest lake, Cave Run, has rentals of pontoons, houseboats and canoes and pedal boats. Go online at www.caverunmarinas.com for more info. Kentucky state parks also has rentals at Greenbo, Yatesville Lake, Paintsville Lake and Grayson Lake. Go online at www.parks.ky.gov.

Just Push Play

HAUNTING

Melissa Stanley was sitting in her bedroom thinking about her dying friend when a neighbor's unused, rusty dinner bell rang loudly, echoing and echoing until it rang right through her.

She knew immediately for whom the bell tolled.

Just a few minutes later, her mom walked into her room, handed her the phone -- her good friend had passed away.

"As long as I lived there I had never heard that bell," said the 28-year-old Huntington resident. "Then, one day -- bang -- the sound emanated through the room and I just stopped, and I knew at that moment that was when he passed. You always heard of the old wives tales of the death bell, and it was somebody I was really close to."

That odd experience two years ago prompted Stanley to rekindle a fascination with life's unexplained, mysterious encounters.

What began as a Yahoo group and chats online, has turned into the two-year-old group, Huntington Paranormal, a band of a dozen or so members who have conducted paranormal investigations at private homes around the Tri-State as well as such area sites as the Keith Albee Theater, the Old Marshall University dorms, the historic State Theater (Point Pleasant), cemeteries in Huntington, Barboursville and Guyandotte, and a couple fruitful visits to Dr. William Grimes' dental office, 1125 20th St., Huntington.

"I have been interested in this stuff for a long time, probably since I was 12 or 13," Stanley said. "I got out of it for a while. Life gets in the way, but when I had that happen a couple of summers ago, it revived my interest and made me wonder, hmmm, are there other people looking to do the same thing?"

Ghost hunters gather

Stanley said that like her, people responded to the group for the same reasons.

They either have had a life-long interest in ghosts and paranormal activities, or have had something happen unexplained that made them want to search for more answers.

"We have one of the guys in the group that when his grandfather passed away he was visited by him," Stanley said. "We all have a story, and most of it starts with close friends or family or someone that grew up in a haunted house."

Not unlike shows on television, such as "Paranormal State" that airs on A&E, the Huntington Paranormal group holes up and sometimes even camps out armed with video recorders, audio recorders and electromagnetic field detectors to see if they can detect anything at a site where a ghost, spirit or odd occurrences have been reported.

"The biggest misconception is that everyone calls us ghostbusters," Stanley said. "We are not ghostbusters. We don't go in and scare out the ghosts like they did in the movie. We go in and take a scientific approach. We take in the equipment and just try and find some kind of proof of something we can't explain."

Going in to investigate

From Gettysburg, Pa., to Guyandotte, the group has taken its equipment to many places looking for evidence of paranormal activity.

A hot-spot for ghost stories is old theaters from Chillicothe's Majestic Theatre that served as a morgue during the flu epidemic during World War I to the Paramount Arts Center in Ashland, long inhabited by Paramount Joe, who even has the coffeehouse named after him.

Here in Huntington, the group checked out the Keith-Albee Performing Arts Center, the historic theater built in 1928.

"There are always stories about the Keith-Albee," Stanley said. "We were really disappointed that we didn't find anything. But, while we were setting up the equipment, we hadn't pushed record and something passed in front of the camera, but it wasn't caught on tape. That is the kind of stuff that happens. You can't make it happen, and you can't predict when it will happen. We have to go back to the Keith because we couldn't confirm any of the stories about the ladies bathroom and that feeling that somebody is standing over your shoulder."

Stanley said they often find some kind of natural cause to explain what has been happening.

"A lot of people's imaginations tend to run away with them," Stanley said. "They don't understand that it could be high EMF readings from unshielded wires that cause them to have experiences. We try and give them some idea of what is going on. We've really only hit on one place that we can really say that we've got consistent things we can't explain."

The doctor's friends are in

While the alleged spirits of the Keith have been elusive, the group hit the paranormal jackpot of sorts at the office of dentist Dr. William Grimes' where there have been countless experiences in this Huntington building on 20th Street.

Grimes said he bought the building -- built about 1901 -- in November 1973.

He and his father began renovating the then duplex into an office and soon realized they weren't alone.

"I bought it in November of 1973, and by December of that year we were pretty convinced that something was going on there that was strange," Grimes said. "My father and I spent hours remodeling, we did everything except for what licensed plumbers and electricians had to do, and we kept hearing loud, very loud noises, like someone absolutely tearing the place apart. We would go to where that happened and nothing would be moved."

Grimes said several members of his family would hear and see things as they were doing the renovations -- things from boards moving to the continued noises.

Initially, Grimes had an alarm system set up at night. It was tripped by microphones and would set off sensors alerting authorities to "someone" on the premise.

"Maybe two times a month on the average they would call me down there thinking someone was down there," Grimes said. "We would come in with a police officer, and nothing would be disturbed. It was such a common occurrence between about 2 and 4 in the morning that finally the police said stop doing this, too many dry runs."

Grimes said they changed the alarm system to a sensor that detects heat and motion and doesn't detect the sounds that continued in the night.

While completing an extensive wallpaper job in the hall and stairwells, Grimes kept sensing someone watching him from outside a bedroom at the top of the stairs.

"I would see things in the stairwell, and I came to the realization that it was a young girl looking at me," Grimes said. "She would step out of the bedroom and stand and look at me. She was raven-haired, had eyes sunken into their sockets, very pale skin and hair matted like she had laid and had been sweating. She would just be quietly staring at me."

Grimes found out from a patient who was related to a former owner of the home, that indeed a child had died in the upstairs bedroom in the 1920s with an acute appendicitis. Her name was Lavina Wall.

She is not the only spirit dressed in period clothes that has shown up at the office.

Grimes has a logbook with dozens of incidents recorded by people, most of which have been his dental assistants, a cleaning lady, and many others, who have from time to time spotted men and women in early 1900s-era clothes hanging around the office then disappearing.

"We just have lots and lots of incidents, and finally I started a log that counted all the major incidents and then try to keep them as up to date as possible and have them write it down in their own words what they saw or heard," Grimes said. "These are not all the incidents, just the few that really seemed to affect people. There's been lots of minor incidents, and there never has been anybody hurt or felt like they were being attacked. It has always been a benevolent type of experience."

Grimes said that while some of his assistants have felt the incidents disconcerting, most have been very open minded about the experiences and they do not try to hide them from anybody.

Grimes even ended up painting a portrait of little Lavina Wall and hanging it at the office.

"Everyone seems to be afraid of the subject," Grimes said. "But once you get past that, everybody started talking about things in their own homes. None of our patients have said, 'You are all a bunch of nuts.' "

Other historic places to explore

While Huntington Paranormal gets a couple calls a month about people wanting them to check out local homes, and or other sites, they have a good, long list of places they want to go check out.

They, of course, want to go back to Dr. Grimes office for a visit.

Most other places on the list are historic places such as the famous Underground Railroad home, The Z.D. Ramsdell House in

Ceredo, The Frederick Hotel in downtown Huntington and the Jenkins Plantation in Greenbottom.

All have their host of ghost stories, like the Jenkins Plantation where people have sworn to have seen children playing in the yard, an old, wiry-haired man standing in the doorway, or suddenly smell pipe tobacco or the smell of fresh bread wafting out of the empty house.

While the group does investigations, it is also out in the community giving some talks.

The group did a presentation before a packed house in March at the Cabell County Public Library downtown, and on Saturday did a presentation about true ghost stories of Huntington, at the Guyandotte Public Library.

In addition to searching for proof of our existence after death, the group also has a mission to help recognize the history of the region.

In fact, the group dresses in period costume as it leads candle-lit walking tours of historic downtown Guyandotte, during the historic Huntington neighborhood's Civil War Days, as well as several other weekends a year.

Stanley, who grew up in Guyandotte, said the free, 45-minute-long tours that will talk about historical homes, ghost sightings and lots of history, is a way to spark interest in new generations about the rich history in the area.

Stanley said that doing the history walks and the talks at the libraries helps folks know they are not alone.

"I think that a lot of people really are interested in the paranormal and always have been," Stanley said. "I have grown up with even my older family members who felt like they saw a ghost or saw something. With shows on television, really everywhere you look it is mainstream and hopefully it helps people just to talk about it more, instead of just having a stigma that they are strange, weird or crazy."

Other ghost hunts and haunts

Here's a look at a few other historic ghost tours in the region.

Mothman: Point Pleasant, Mason County: Nearly 40 years later, the flame of the Mothman legend continues to attract believers, skeptics and the curious. Visit the Mothman Museum and other super, natural attractions in Point Pleasant. A limited number of guided bus tours to the TNT area are set for specific Saturdays During the trip, your tour guide will narrate the pivotal locations and scenes of Mothman encounters. Call 304-675-3844 to arrange for a guided tour or visitwww.mothmanlives.com.

Haunted Columbus: Built in 1882, the historic and one-of-a-kind Lofts Hotel, located in downtown's Arena District. The Lofts is a featured site on the Columbus Landmarks Association "Haunted Columbus's Best of 20 Years Bus Tour." Call 614-461-2663 or 800-73LOFTS or by visitingwww.55lofts.com.

Haunted Parkersburg: Named the number 10 most popular ghost tour in the nation in 2008 by the Haunted America Tours, this historical walk covers ghosts and hauntings and tales of a Scottish Banshees, red-eyed portents of doom attached to certain Irish and Scottish clans, and of course, the stories of Indrid Cold, featured in the "Mothman Prophecies." The tours begin at the Blennerhassett Hotel in downtown Parkersburg. Go online at www.hauntedparkersburg.com.

Prison Ghost Tours: The famous Ohio State Reformatory in Mansfield, Ohio, hosts overnight ghost hunt tours. Built in 1886, the prison held prisoners for 94 years. On the National Register of Historic Places, the prison has been featured in such films as "Shawshank Redemption." Go online at www.mrps.org or call 800-642-8282.

Moundsville Prison's All Night Ghost Hunts: At Moundsville, W.Va., roam the gothic structure that once housed many of the nation's most dangerous criminals. Walk with experienced paranormal investigators as they explore the spirits from the darker side of humanity. Ghost Hunts are open to the public, age 18 years and up. From April through November, you can experience daylight tours or call to book a night tour. Contact 304-845-6200, www.wvpentours.com.

North Bend Rail Trail Ghost Walk: In Cairo, Ritchie County:

Take a slow walk into the dark night on the North Bend Rail Trail. The flat walk is easy on your feet; the ghostly tales such as the Phantom of Silver Run chilling on your spine. The North Bend Rail Trail is open to pedestrians, equestrians and bicyclists year round. Contact R. C. Marshall Hardware Co., Cairo, 304-628-3321.

Ghost Tours of Lewisburg: Greenbrier County: Take a candlelight tour of haunted homes and sites in the Historic District of Lewisburg. Choose from The Cemetery, The Mansions or the Carnegie Hall Tour. Contact John Luckton 304-256-TOUR (8687).

Trans Allegheny Lunatic Asylum: Formerly Weston State Hospital in Lewis County. Reported paranormal activity makes this haunted pre-Civil War hospital a "must" for every ghost hunter. Ghost hunts are offered year round. Heritage tours are offered seasonally. Call to arrange private tours. For information on private tours or special events contact Rebecca Jordan at 304-269-5070 or visit their Web site at www.trans-alleghenylunaticasylum.com.

Ghost Tours of Beckley, Raleigh County: See turn-of-the-century haunted sites, including the Raleigh County Courthouse, Coal Baron Mansions, and The 1931 Historic Soldiers and Sailors Theatre (interior tour). Contact John Luckton at 304-256-TOUR (8687).

Just Push Play

BIKING

He might not be a mailman, but Joel Mullins boldly treks through rain and snow, dark and cold, tropical heat and humidity, just to get his pedal on.

A 27-year-old cook at Cabell-Huntington Hospital, Mullins has been to every monthly Critical Mass Huntington ride since the free six-mile community bicycle event began in July 2009.

Now the organizer of the Critical Mass Huntington, Mullins wants all bikes and skateboards on deck at 6:30 p.m. Friday, July 20, at the Ritter Park fountain as the group celebrates its third anniversary with a festive group ride around the city.

Mullins said they hope to break the record of 140 participants that was set last July by the group, started by Huntington native and former NYC deejay Jesse Clark when he moved back from New York where he did Critical Mass in Brooklyn and Manhattan.

Mullins, who has not missed a Critical Mass said every one has its own flavor and fun, but it was hard to beat last July when the city's cyclists rolled out large for the anniversary.

"Once we got started I was up at the front of the group and I looked back on a line of cyclists maybe two abreast that stretched out for about half a mile," Mullins said. "That was really impressive."

Mullins said it is hard to quantify but he feels like the festive and safe monthly event, usually led by HPD's burgeoning number of officers certified on bikes, has encouraged more cycling in the city.

"When you come out and see 100 or more people on their bikes and the broad range of demographics that it attracts you realize it is more socially acceptable now and it's cool," Mullins said. "I know I have really noticed that more people are riding in general and I think that has helped out. I am not sure how much of an impact this has but I know more people are riding more often which is really encouraging."

Mullins, who has been riding for about nine years, said it was after the second Critical Mass that he began commuting to work.

"I started out riding for transportation but really got to enjoy it after a while and I started losing weight and getting in shape," said Mullins who went from barely riding a mountain bike to a hybrid (road bike tires on a mountain bike frame), to a road bike.

"After the second mass that we had in August (2009) I was going to start commuting to work and with a few exceptions I have been riding my bike to work every day for three years," Mullins said. "It really was a natural progression and that is why I think Critical Mass every month is important. I want people to feel they can have that sort of progression."

Along with the growth of Critical Mass, Huntington has been embracing its bike culture. Just this year, the city striped some bike lanes in downtown, the Paul Ambrose Trail to Health or (PATH) is seeing progress, and events such as Tour de Path and the upcoming Buns on Bikes (as part of the WV Hotdog Festival) are also seeing large numbers of riders.

And bicycling family, Stacy Bisker and Brent Patterson have brought the Kidical Mass (entry and kid level) bicycle ride to Huntington, as well as organizing other themed cycling rides in the city.

Mullins said the collective makes Huntington -- already a good, mostly-flat city to ride in -- that much safer.

"The biggest thing for me is that drivers recognize that they are going to see people on bikes," Mullins said. "If you don't know to look out for them it may come as a shock or surprise and drivers are more likely to behave erratically if all of a sudden there is a cyclist. It definitely has improved now that there are less random people riding. I hardly ever get hassled, it's mellowed out significantly. Just anecdotally, Huntington is better off than a lot of bigger cities. There is not as much traffic and it's easier to avoid it. Just stay off 5th and 3rd avenues and 8th Street for the most part and you can really pick your route to go wherever you want to go and you'll be fine."

Mullins, who has been doing some bicycle apprentice work with his brother David who manages Jeff's Bike Shop on 8th Street, said

he hopes folks continue to support and grow the event that is one of the best attended Critical Mass events in the region.

"I know Charleston had a massive drop-off in their Critical Mass and we haven't had less than a dozen even in the winter months," Mullins said. "They sometimes can't get a dozen in the summer. I don't want that to happen here. I want people to see there are people riding every day and that Critical Mass is going to be there and be consistent. They have to know they can count on it and that it is a really big deal. That is why I keep coming back.

Huntington Critical Mass: Held since July 2009, the Huntington Critical Mass takes place on the third Friday of every month at 6:30 p.m. at the Ritter Park fountain. Cycliststravel about six miles during the event open to any area cyclists and skateboarders. Go online at www.facebook.com/huntingtoncriticalmass

Kenova Critical Mass: Kenova Critical Mass takes place at 6:30 p.m. on the last Friday of every month. Meet at the Kenova Town Square gazebo and take an easy paced six-mile ride around the city. Skateboarders and roller skaters also welcome. For more information about Critical Mass Kenova, call Mandy Jordan at 304-939-2083, email mandyjordan59@yahoo.com and check out their Facebook page.

PATH: The Paul Ambrose Trail for Health or PATH has both Share the Road signage and trails that connect Huntington with safe bicycling and running routes.

Grab a Huntington Bike Map and head out to take in some of the PATH, like the floodwall portion west of Harris Riverfront Park, the Ritter Park PATH that connects to Harveytown Park, the Guyandotte to Alitzer route along Riverside Drive, or try and cycle the entire PATH (about 30 miles), which can be done in a long afternoon.

Get a map at the Cabell Huntington Convention and Visitors Bureau, Jeff's Bikes and Huntington Cycle and Sport.

Go online at www.paulambrosetrail.org/ for more info about the trail and the annual Tour de PATH.

Buns on Bikes: Part of the WV Hot dog Festival since 2009, Buns on Bikes is a family-friendly bicycle ride that starts and ends at Pullman Square with a ride to the Ritter Park Memorial Arch and back. Proceeds go to the Hoops Family Children's Hospital at Cabell Huntington Hospital.

Kidical Mass: A kids and family-themed bicycle group ride. Past rides in Huntington include the annual holiday lights ride, a geocaching ride and other fun themed rides.

Just Push Play

ON THE CHEAP

Here are just a few ideas for saving money on trips, as well as some inexpensive and free things to check out here in the Tri-State.

Pack a lunch: Bring healthy snacks and water from home for the road. It's cheaper and much healthier since you're not tempted to hit fast-food joints along the way. Also, don't just eat your lunch in the car; find a state park or playground along the way to stop. Some of the most interesting trips can be those in which we stop somewhere amazing on the way to or from the actual destination. Also, some places such as zoos and amusement parks will let folks bring in picnics. Check before you go.

Get free audio book downloads at the library: I'm not really a fan of zoning the kids out to video (but hey, if it works for you, then by any means necessary to make the kids chill on a long trip). That said, an alternative is that you can download free audio books from the Cabell County Public Library or your local library. You also can get videos as well. Go online at www.cabell.lib.wv.us.

Stay with family and friends: Motel 6 will leave the light on for you, but family and friends living in cool nearby cities, will even make you dinner. This is a great way to keep in touch with your wonderful circle of friends that meant to come visit you, but never found the time. Also, be sure and look at non-chain options as well. We've found some great deals and cool places staying at mom-and-pop lodging.

Go with a crew: Things are always cheaper when you go with a group. Get a handful of friends or family with your church, scouts or social network, to rent a cabin, get group tickets to an amusement park or to do a group activity for a weekend. In years past we enjoyed a unique Scout overnight trip staying all night at the Cincinnati Zoo. It was an inexpensive but priceless experience.

Share meals: One of the obvious contributors to the obesity epidemic is portion sizes and nearly every restaurant slaps down Shaq-sized meals in front of one person. Cut the calories and the cost by buying one meal to split for adults and one to split for two kids.

Off-peak times: Travel during the off-season to snag some great deals. In West Virginia, you can get some awesome deals and good conditions by skiing in March and December, and you can have the zoos to yourself in Cincinnati, Columbus or Louisville by visiting in the winter.

Festivals, festivals, festivals: Our area is packed with great festivals. Many have free admission and/or free admission for kids. For expensive multi-day music fests, inquire about being a volunteer. Often volunteers get free passes and great access to these fests.

Get the local publication: Before you head out to a nearby city, check out their newspaper or special publications. You can unearth some awesome, free shows that only the locals know about. It may cost you 50 cents but being in the know and exploring like a local is priceless.

Explore at home: There's tons of free exploring to be done in our immediate area with kids. Check out the new playgrounds at Harveytown Park and Ritter Park, or the rock-climbing wall at Marshall's new recreation center. There are also some cheap and free cave trips at nearby Carter Caves State Park, free disc golf courses at Huntington's Rotary Park, and at Ashland's Armco Park, as well as great hiking at such spots as Beech Fork State Park, Lake Vesuvius, and Yatesville Lake. There are free movies shown at the Cabell County and Boyd County Public libraries and Tuesday's are free at the Huntington Museum of Art. And for kids who love to be on their smart phones, geocaching is a great, free adventure.

On the way: Instead of just driving as fast as you can to your destination, find some cool things to stop off and see along the way, like interesting state parks. We used the website (www.roadtrippers.com) to locate some amazing places like Rickett's Glen in eastern Pa., that literally had 20 waterfalls in a three mile hike.

Just Push Play

GEOCACHING

The marquee on the historic Keith-Albee Performing Arts Center read, "Welcome Geocachers."

Don't worry, that was not another new band you don't know about -- that was just a sign letting people know the weekend was to be chock full of geocaching adventure.

People tried the high-tech treasure hunt called geocaching during the weekend of March 14-15, 2014 as Huntington hosted the first Cabell County Geotrail with cachers from around the country.

Sponsored by the Cabell-Huntington Convention and Visitors Bureau, the free weekend of events had folks - armed with the Geocaching.com Smart Phone app or a GPS - go on this scavenger hunt to find 15 caches hidden at sites all over the county by following GPS coordinates to the sites.

People who got all 15 caches received a special commemorative Geocoin that featured the Marshall Memorial fountain on one side and the Heritage Station train on the other side.

More than 300 people came from Delaware to Illinois and from New York to North Carolina and all points in between. Included in that number is some of the world's best geocachers, including folks from Cincinnati who have logged 60,000 finds and New Yorkers who have gone over the 48,000 mark.

For "muggles" or folks who don't cache, Geocaching was started in Portland, Ore., and Seattle, Wash., in 2000. Called the game "where you are the search engine," Geocaching was first attempted solely on GPS units, but it exploded as that technology became available in smartphones.

Geocaching has grown to include nearly 2,331,210 caches (or small hidden boxes filled with various little treasures for the taking) and more than six million geocachers worldwide.

In the Tri-State, within a 50-mile radius of Huntington, there are more than 9,000 geocaches hiding out in parks, cemeteries and important spots such as the Marshall plane crash site. Expert cachers such as Steve and Debbie Adkins, who've found more than 2,030 caches in 11 states, helped design the trail of caches, which will still is around and ready to be found. Also working on the design was Bobby Wintz.

"The trail itself is phenomenal -- we have so many unique hides," Adkins said. "None are too hidden but some are a little gadgety, and you have to use your head a little bit to find them. Every container is a different container, and we took you to some good spots in the county."

Adkins said the beauty of caching is that it leads participants to unique historical, geological or quirky local interest sites most often. It is during those visits and afterward that he's found he's picked up a continuing education about places in these United States.

One of his favorite sites was Sheldon Church in Beaufort County, S.C. The church was burned in the Revolutionary War, rebuilt and then fell under the flame of Gen. Sherman during the Civil War.

"It was one of the most unusual places we've been," Adkins said. "History is right under your nose, and this does such a good job of teaching history not just to kids, but it is educational for adults and older people, too. I have learned so much from doing it, and there are so many memories that you make with your family and friends that are priceless."

From the CVB's standpoint, geocaching is an inexpensive, creative and physically active way to draw in more tourists and to get local residents to treat the Tri-State like tourists, taking them on a trail of rediscovery of local stories and special places.

"We identify it as attracting new visitors who wouldn't normally come here," said one of the trail organizers, Jake Sharp, who was with the CVB. "Secondly, we see it as exciting locals and giving them something new and different to do. It gives local people a chance to explore their home, because they are doing it in a way that they would not do otherwise. We get people all of the time who don't know anything about Blenko Glass or Heritage Farm or who haven't been to Camden Park."

Just Push Play

ZIPLINING

The new color-splashed billboards just put up in Canaan Valley say it all, Timberline -- "Ski, Zip."

West Virginia's only family-owned ski resort, Timberline Four Seasons Resort in Davis, W.Va., has joined a growing number of ski resorts around the country installing ziplines as an added seasonal attraction.

Just opened in 2014, the zipline attraction can have up to four people zipping side-by-side 1,000 feet past the four-story Timberline Lodge with a bird's eye view of the lodge and several converging ski trails.

Launched from a massive tower 50 feet in the air, the zipline gently slopes down with riders traveling at speeds at up to 25 miles an hour before braking and landing at a 35-foot-high tower that sits near one of the resort's ski lifts and within view of the resort's ski-in, ski-out Timberline Hotel.

Already tested out by Timberline CEO Fred Herz, who lives in Milton, and Tom Blanzy, general manager at Timberline, the ziplines are now being opened to the public with the recent subzero Arctic temperatures in the rearview mirror.

The first four-person zip in the state opened to the general public Saturday, Jan. 25, 2014. The new attraction is one of only a couple four-person zipline attractions in the East (Wildcat Mountain in New Hampshire has a four-person zipline).

Herz said after the opening, regular hours will be established for the zipline attraction, which will not run during ski season but during the rest of the year.

Blanzy, the long-time resort manager, said while the resort, which sits up against the expansive Dolly Sods Wilderness Area, is already known for off-season adventures including mountain biking, hiking and horseback riding, the ziplines add another great reason to come and stay and play at Timberline.

"We hope it is going to be the start of some additional things of that nature so we can develop more of the year-round activities and the adventures sports, where it is not just a zipline but a full program of safe skills where people can test their courage in a good environment," Blanzy said. "One of our company's slogans is inner quest, and this does challenge yourself. I am not the greatest person when it comes to heights. Logically I know it is very safe but intuitively I might be asking why am I doing this, but that explores a part of me that is probably good."

The soft-spoken Blanzy, isn't just all talk when it comes to testing courage.

After some coaxing, he was one of the first handful of folks to cowboy up and climb the 50-foot tower for a breathtaking ride.

"When you are up there and looking over the edge you are thinking what do I do now, I'm not going to go back but personally my take on it was I am going to just look at the rope this is the part that I am trusting in," Blanzy said speaking of the industrial cables that connect the towers. "I have faith in the people who built this and I am just going to look at the rope. I lifted up my feet and there I went. It was a really good adrenaline rush and after a few seconds I was like this is good, I am still alive and then I had the courage to look around and that was the good part of it, and when you hit the brake at the end it has a nice little swing to it."

Seen from every level of Timberline's lodge, including the upstairs restaurant, Timber's Pub, the zipline couldn't be in a more visible place as nearly everyone can see the action.

"Originally I didn't know if it was a good idea or not to put it so near the lodge but then the more I thought about it, and the more other people looked at it, we were like 'yeah this is where we should put it because this is where all of the activity is,'" Blanzy said. "Eventually we could also expand off of this and put it an area where we could put a tubing park and where we have a significant amount of property, but as far as this goes now, you have this center of activity that is all right here."

Blanzy said placing the zip in such a visible spot gives folks the thought that maybe they could try the zip, and people who are at the lodge just hanging out something to watch as well from the giant bank of lodge windows.

"That is what is so good about Timberline you are not isolated from all of the activity that is going on," Blanzy said. "It is all coming in right here and people feel like they are a part of it. People might not ski or mountain bike but they might do this so it is going to be part of an overall experience. So we are hoping that we can bring some non-skiers here too. It is safe and it is fun."

Herz said they saw the zipline, which can accommodate riders from 60 to 300 pounds, as a great additional attraction for visitors.

"It's a unique thing to have family and friends zipping together," Herz said. "We're not aware of many other four parallel line ziplines so it is unique in the Eastern United States. I thought this would be a very good addition for the Boy Scout program. We do such a large number of Scouts each year and during the evening hours, they don't ski as much and we do have some things they can do. They watch movies in the lodge and limited video games and they'll hang out and play board games but this is something that will really appeal to that group."

Blanzy said he and Herz and Timberline's founder Doc Reichle began talking about adding a zipline last spring and they turned to an expert in the area, John Hall of Nelson Rocks Preserve to install the $250,000 towers and lines and to run it as a year-round concession.

Located south of Seneca Rocks, Nelson Rocks features a zipline tour, as well as Via Ferrata, a -mile-long guided, self-belayed climbing adventure.

After talking to several builders, Blanzy, said the Nelson Rocks crew was at, and local choice for building the new high-adventure draw.

"He's got a really nice place over by Nelson Rocks and he's into a lot of different things with his business," Blanzy said. "He built a pretty good zipline down in Puerto Rico and he was instrumental, along with the folks in the New River Gorge, in developing the state statute in operation of ziplines. He has an excellent group and staff that he works with everyone from engineers and guides to accounting and marketing. He has a very well-known organization and we hope to do further things with this group to provide more year-round amenities."

Providing more year-round amenities, is definitely a trend hitting ski resorts across the States. USA Today wrote a summer 2013 story highlighting the new plethora of off-season adventures, everything from mountain coasters to ziplines that now draw in folks to ski areas year-round.

That story highlighted the well-established Park City Mountain Resort zipline tour, and other resources show that the zipline trend is hitting the East Coast, as there are now three ziplines at Vermont ski areas, two in Maine and six in New Hampshire, with Bretton Woods' featuring a 10-line zipline tour across its mountain.

In West Virginia, where there are five ski areas, Timberline joined the largest resort, Snowshoe Mountain, as the second resort to put in a zip. Snowshoe put in a zipline through its mountaintop village last year.

Blanzy said the key is now to get out the word and to let folks know that Timberline and the Canaan Valley area has added one more attraction to its already packed list.

"We've got a lot of people talking about it and everyone here from the Convention and Visitors Bureau to all of the social media is excited about it," Blanzy said. "We're just trying to get everyone aware that this is the start of something really good here. We appreciate the fact that is here and it is a big investment for John. We just want people to be able to come here and enjoy themselves and come back. If they do that we will all be happy and we will all benefit from that. When you go on vacation people want things to do and they want to relax and this is part of providing more of that."

Let's Go Trippin: Ziplining

WHAT IS IT: The state's first four-person side-by-side Zipline. The new zip is 50 foot high, runs for 1,000 feet in front of the Timberline Four Seasons Resort lodge. Riders reach speeds of up to 25 miles an hour.

WHERE IS IT: Timberline Four Seasons Resort, Davis. W.Va.

WHO CAN GO? Riders must be between 60 and 300 pounds, and depending on the wind conditions, the minimum weight. Wind/weather may at times require increased minimum weight requirements for safety and operation.

WHO BUILT IT? John Hall and the folks at Via Ferrata at Nelson Rocks Preserve. Located south of Seneca Rocks that high adventure outdoor recreation area features a zipline tour, as well as Via Ferrata, a 3/4-mile-long guided self belayed climbing adventure for folks 13 and up. They've also built ziplines in Puerto Rico.

CONTACT: You can find out more info at Timberline's web site at www.timberlineresort.com and check out Timberline on Facebook and Twitter @Tline. You can also call 1-800-SNOWING for more info.

Other Cool Places to Zipline

Cooper Family Farms: The Maize at Cooper Farms in Milton, W.Va., put in a zipline course over the corn maze. The course is made up of three towers (the highest being 80+ feet, nick named "Stairway to Heaven") and three zip runs with over 1,500 feet of fast flying fun. Cost is $12 for a single course pass and $20 for a twice through pass. Rider weight limits are 80 pounds to 260. Go online at www.cooperfamilyfarms.net for more info.

Highline At Carter Caves: Friends of Carter Caves puts up a highline that runs on select weekends as well as during the Winter Adventure Weekend at Carter Caves State Resort Park. The highline is set up near Smoky Bridge, a large natural bridge at the park. The phone number for the park is 1-800-325-0059.

Zipline Safari Tour: Located in Cumberland, Ohio, at The Wilds, the largest conservation facility in North America, enjoy the Wilds from an aerial perspective. Led by two professionally trained guides, this 2 ½ hour zipline safari tour consists of 10 ziplines built on a series of observation platforms overlooking various rare and endangered animal species that are home to the Wilds. Go online at www.zipthewilds.com for more info.

TreeTops Canopy Tour: Located at Adventures in the Gorge in Lansing, W.Va., TreeTops is considered one of the top 10 zipline courses in the U.S., with 10 zips, five cable bridges, overviews of Mill Creek and one rappel station. There's also the high speed Gravity ziplines at Adventures as well. Go online at www.adventuresonthegorge.com for more info.

Hocking Hills Canopy Tours: Located at Hocking Hills, Ohio, near Logan, Ohio in southern Ohio. This is Ohio's first ziplines. New is the X Tour, a three-hour, 11-zip tour that includes a combo of trees and towers and has you zipping into a hidden recessed cave, crossing the Hocking River twice and more. Go online at www.hockinghillscanopytour.com

Red River Gorge Zipline: Five ziplines, canopy bridges, dual zips and some zips set more than 300 feet above the Gorge. Go online at www.redrivergorgezipline.com.

Mega Zips: One of the world's only underground zipline courses has six underground ziplines, including a dual racing zip, two bridge and more at Mega Cavern in Louisville. Go online at www.louisvillemegacavern.com

Nelson Rocks Outdoor Center: A canopy course with 12 ziplines, three sky bridges and a 40-foot rappel at Nelson Rocks near Seneca Rock in Circleville, W.Va. Contact @NelsonRocksOutdoorCenter.com or call 877-435-4842.

Index

A

Abrahamson, 82
Abrams, 108
A Christmas Story House, 101, 107
Adventures On The Gorge, 45, 183
Adventure West Virginia, 45
Airboat, 95, 135, 141, 160
Alitzer, 172
Allegheny, 70-71, 118, 168
Allegiant, 141, 146
Ansted, 83
Appomattox, 145
Aquarium, 112, 115, 127-130
Aracoma, 122
Arboretum, 56
Ashland, 14-15, 26, 33, 46, 60, 88, 107, 118, 160, 163, 174
Astroland, 65
Athens, 31, 88
Augusta, 14
Avampato, 46, 60
Aviation, 46

B

B and B Riverboats, 160
Babcock, 59
Backpacking, 31
Bahia, 136, 142

Bannerman, 35
Barboursville, 47, 91, 161
Bardstown, 122
Barn, 9, 11, 18-19, 46, 94
Beartown State Park, 31, 52, 54-55, 58
Beckley, 99-100, 119, 122, 168
Beech Fork, 28, 59, 69, 174
Beer, 79, 87-88, 134, 153
Bellevue, 35
Bellville, 132
Belmont, 149
Belpre, 160
Berdawn, 84
Bigfoot, 79
Billy Bobs, 47
biplane, 46, 70
birds, 20, 114, 135
Blackwater, 52, 59, 71, 75, 100
BlackwaterFalls, 75, 100
Blenko, 80, 176
Blennerhassett, 15, 160, 167
Bluefield, 81, 86
Bluegrass, 7, 57, 60, 80, 121
Bluestone, 81
Boardwalk, 27, 31, 55, 57, 75, 98, 135, 141
Boyd, 174
Boylin, 64-66, 68
Boylins, 65
Bramwell, 3, 81-86
Brandenburg, 36
breweries, 71, 84-85, 87-88
Bridgeton, 67
bridgewalk, 26

ABOUT THE AUTHOR AND PHOTOGRAPHER

Dave Lavender is a life-long Tri-Stater, born and raised in Franklin Furnace, Ohio. Educated at Shawnee State University and the University of Kentucky, Dave has been a working journalist for more than 20 years, and has been writing and living the past 15 years in Huntington, W.Va.

Dave is a writer for The Herald-Dispatch and is twice weekly featured on the radio. He likes to whistle while bicycling to work.

Toril Lavender was born in Tucson, Arizona and raised in Fayetteville, New York. A graduate of Syracuse University, Toril was a national award-winning photographer for Gannett and a freelancer for such publications as The Washington Post.

Toril is the owner of Lavender Photography, which specializes in wedding and portrait photography. She has had art shows in Maine and West Virginia and her photo work has been featured in West Virginia Living and Tri-State Living.

42687959R00110

Made in the USA
Charleston, SC
03 June 2015